Contents

"If a wormhole doesn't include the possibility of going backward in time, it's not as close to reality."

— Stephen Hawking

1. Introduction: The Lure of the Cosmic Bridge

Imagine standing on the precipice of existence, looking into a cosmic doorway that could transport you not only across the vast stellar expanses but also into realms unfathomable. The idea of wormhole travel has captured the imaginations of both scientists and storytellers alike, promising a journey beyond the limits of time and space. Yet, how pragmatic is this captivating concept?

In this book, "To Infinity and Beyond: The Science and Fiction of Wormhole Travel," we will embark on a fascinating voyage into the mysterious world of wormholes. We will explore not only the scientific principles that suggest wormholes might exist but also the cultural and literary implications of such a profound possibility.

From the latest research in quantum physics and the Einstein-Rosen Bridge to its depictions in classic and contemporary science fiction, this work seeks to unravel the rich tapestry of wormhole lore. Whether you're a seasoned science enthusiast or a curious reader stepping into the cosmic unknown for the first time, this journey is sure to intrigue, inform, and inspire.

2. Understanding Wormholes: The Basics

2.1. What is a Wormhole?

A wormhole is a theoretical construct in the realm of physics that functions as a tunnel-like structure connecting two separate points in spacetime. In simple terms, think of it as a shortcut through the fabric of the universe. The concept of a wormhole finds its roots in the theories of both general relativity and quantum mechanics, and it has significant implications for our understanding of the very nature of space and time.

The idea was first put forward in 1935 by renowned physicists Albert Einstein and Nathan Rosen, who proposed what is now referred to as the Einstein-Rosen Bridge. This conceptualization was founded on the principles of general relativity, which posits that mass and energy can warp spacetime, creating curves within the fabric of the universe. Their work illustrated how one could theoretically link two distinct points in space through a 'bridge,' hence the term "bridge" in their naming. The Einstein-Rosen Bridge suggests a connection between black holes, implying that a black hole in one part of the universe could hypothetically lead to a different point in spacetime, creating a route for potential traversal.

While wormholes are often depicted in popular media as portals for time travel or instantaneous travel across vast distances, the physics behind them is determinant on their stability and properties. A quintessential characteristic of a wormhole is that it consists of two mouths connected by a throat. The mouths are the openings, where one could theoretically enter and exit, and the throat serves as the conduit. The geometry of a wormhole can be incredibly complex, shaped by the distribution of mass and energy around it and potentially influenced by factors like exotic matter, which has negative energy density—a necessity to keep the wormhole from collapsing under gravitational forces.

The exploration of wormholes raises major biological, physical, and philosophical questions: What happens if we were to enter one?

Would we emerge unscathed on the other side, and if we could indeed travel through a wormhole, what might it mean for our understanding of time and causality? These questions place wormholes at the intersection of scientific inquiry and human imagination.

Indeed, while the theories suggest that wormholes could exist, actual proof remains elusive. The laws of physics as we currently understand them create substantial hurdles regarding their formation, stability, and usability for travel. Current theories propose that if wormholes do exist, they would likely be incredibly tiny and highly unstable, making it virtually impossible for humans to traverse them or even observe them directly.

The nature of wormholes invites profound speculation. Could they serve as bridges to alternate universes, allowing for travel not just through space, but possibly through time? This notion is enticing to theoretical physicists, and it also captivates writers of science fiction, who have adopted the concept in various narratives. Through works of literature and cinema, wormholes have become synonymous with boundless exploration and potential, igniting wonder about whether they could one day be a reality.

Within the broader context of our ongoing quest for knowledge, the exploration of wormholes reflects humanity's enduring desire to transcend limitations and reach for the stars. The notion of manipulating spacetime opens up dizzying possibilities that resonate deeply within both our scientific understanding and our narratives, challenging us to think beyond what is currently known. As research continues in the fields of astrophysics and quantum mechanics, mathematicians and physicists remain hopeful that one day, these elusive cosmic structures might transform from abstract mathematical solutions to tangible realities.

Thus, the quest to understand what a wormhole is not only pertains to the science itself but also to the fabric of the universe, where imagination and scientific inquiry converge in our pursuit of knowledge and exploration. It leaves us gazing into the cosmos, pondering the mysteries that await—ready to step into the unknown, if only we can find the right doorway beyond the stars.

2.2. The Physics Behind the Concept

The exploration of wormholes is intricately tied to the multifaceted principles of physics, particularly the theories of general relativity and the intertwined nature of spacetime. At the core of this scientific framework lies the notion that the universe is not simply a backdrop where events transpire, but rather a dynamic fabric that can be warped and manipulated by mass and energy. According to Einstein's groundbreaking theory of general relativity, the presence of mass distorts spacetime, creating curves that dictate the movement of objects. This insight is fundamental in understanding how wormholes—a hypothetical construct originating from this relativistic perspective—might exist and function.

To comprehend wormholes more deeply, one must first grasp the concept of spacetime itself. Traditionally, space and time have been treated as separate entities; however, the theory of general relativity posits that they are interwoven into a single continuum. In this model, the position of an object in space is inherently linked to its position in time. The implications of this merger provide a framework for considering how wormholes could theoretically serve as shortcuts in this continuum. Imagine folding a two-dimensional sheet of paper, representing space, so that two distant points touch each other. The crease symbolizes a wormhole, connecting two separate points in spacetime. This visualization of folding highlights how one could traverse vast distances in an instant, bypassing the traditional constraints of traveling through space.

The foundational mathematics of general relativity introduces a set of equations known as the Einstein Field Equations, which describe how matter and energy shape the curvature of spacetime. When applied to certain solutions within these equations, intriguing possibilities emerge, including the mathematical modeling of wormholes. The structure of a wormhole is often visualized as consisting of two "mouths" hooked by a "throat," analogous to a tunnel with entrances on either end. In specific solutions, notably the Schwarzschild solution, the throat manifests as a bridge between these mouths, enabling theoretical travel from one point in the universe to another.

However, the theoretical nature of wormholes leads to significant challenges, primarily around their stability and traversability. The energy conditions governing spacetime suggest that typical forms of matter are insufficient to sustain a stable wormhole. To prevent it from collapsing under gravitational forces, exotic matter—characterized by a negative energy density—would be required. This necessity leads to compelling inquiries within the realms of quantum mechanics, particularly concerning its potential to offer insights into states of matter that are otherwise inconceivable. The so-called "exotic" properties of such matter would counterbalance gravitational attraction at the throat, thus maintaining the wormhole's structure.

Quantum mechanics plays a vital role in our conceptualization of wormholes, especially through its implications regarding spacetime fluctuations. At the quantum scale, the fabric of spacetime exhibits a peculiar behavior, where continuous fluctuations might give rise to transient micro-wormholes. These fluctuations suggest that on an infinitesimal scale, wormholes may not only exist theoretically but emerge spontaneously, representing potential gateways to deeper insights into the universe. The relationship between these quantum phenomena and macroscopic wormholes invites intriguing questions about the very nature of reality and the fundamental forces at play in defining our universe.

As scientific inquiry into these phenomena continues, notable contributions by physicists such as Kip Thorne and others have propelled the discourse surrounding traversable wormholes forward. Thorne, in particular, laid foundational groundwork by contemplating the implications of negative energy and how it might be harnessed in future experiments. His work also extends into speculative constructs that bridge the gap between theoretical physics and practical applications, continuously pushing the boundaries of understanding.

The discussion of wormholes inevitably leads to paradoxes, particularly concerning time travel. The intersection of general relativity and quantum mechanics hints at the existence of closed timelike curves —paths in spacetime that return to the starting point in time, potentially allowing for travel into the past. Such ramifications generate profound philosophical inquiries about causality and the fabric of reality, further intensifying the intrigue associated with wormhole research.

In conclusion, the physics behind wormholes presents a fascinating interplay of general relativity and quantum mechanics, rich in theoretical potential yet laden with challenges. As researchers delve deeper into the mathematics and implications of wormholes, the boundaries of our understanding stretch and bend, much like the spacetime they traverse. The continued exploration of these cosmic bridges not only serves to expand our scientific horizon but also invites contemplation into the philosophical realms of existence, time, and the very nature of the universe itself. The quest for understanding wormholes epitomizes humanity's enduring pursuit of knowledge and our fascination with the cosmos, beckoning us to dream of the extraordinary possibilities that lie just beyond our reach.

2.3. Historical Context and Discovery

In the grand tapestry of scientific thought, the concept of wormholes emerges as a fascinating thread interwoven with significant historical milestones and key personalities. Originating from deep within the intricacies of theoretical physics, the idea of a shortcut through the cosmos wasn't merely a whimsical notion; it evolved through rigorous academic discourse and bold conjectures presented by renowned thinkers. This exploration delves into how wormholes transitioned from theoretical abstractions to widely recognized symbols of cosmic possibility, fervently debated among scientists and cherished by imaginations across the globe.

The genesis of wormhole theory can be traced back to the early 20th century, a period bursting with revolutionary ideas in physics. Albert Einstein's formulation of the theory of general relativity in

1915 provided a fresh perspective on gravity and confirmed that mass and energy could bend the fabric of spacetime. However, it was not until 1935 that the concept of the wormhole truly took shape, arising from the minds of Einstein and his colleague Nathan Rosen. Together, they proposed what became known as the Einstein-Rosen Bridge, a theoretical structure that serves as a bridge between different points in spacetime. This groundbreaking paper not only introduced the ideas of wormhole connections but also challenged the established understanding of the universe's fabric, suggesting that spacetime is far more complex than previously conceived.

The flow of scientific discovery continued with significant contributions from contemporaries and successors of Einstein and Rosen. For instance, in the 1960s and 1970s, physicists such as John Archibald Wheeler and Kip Thorne further fleshed out the mechanics of wormholes and their implications. Wheeler popularized the notion of "wormholes" itself whereas Thorne, known for his work on the nature of black holes and gravitational waves, began exploring the practical aspects of traversable wormholes. Thorne's meticulous dedication to theoretical groundwork laid the foundation for future scientists to investigate the stability and potential realities of wormholes.

A pivotal moment in the historical context of wormhole exploration occurred in 1988, when Kip Thorne and his collaborators showed that it might be possible to create stable wormholes under certain conditions. They proposed that these exotic constructions could be maintained with the use of theoretically conceivable "exotic matter," a type of matter with negative energy density that goes against the conventional understanding of mass-energy equivalence. This groundbreaking exploration not only captivated physicists but also captured the interest of the broader public, cementing wormholes in the collective consciousness as potential pathways through the cosmos.

Throughout the years, the discussion of wormholes expanded beyond the realm of academia, penetrating popular culture and a myriad of science fiction narratives. The idea of these cosmic shortcuts captured imaginations, leading to their portrayal in films, literature, and television, portraying the thrilling possibilities of interstellar travel. Iconic literary works and cinematic masterpieces have taken creative liberties with the concept, including movies like "Interstellar," which utilized insights from Thorne's research to craft a gripping narrative about time dilation and the interplay of love, loss, and the vast unknowns of space.

As we dig deeper into the historical context, it becomes evident that the dialogue surrounding wormholes is laced with a continuous cycle of conjecture and skepticism. The idea has faced criticism and rigorous debates concerning the paradoxes of time travel and the stability of such structures. Constants in this conversation include the questions of whether traversable wormholes could ever be realized and the ethical implications orbiting their potential existence. The scientific community remains divided, with theorists continuing to propose models while empirical proof remains tantalizingly out of reach.

Despite these debates, the allure of wormholes resonates as both a scientific endeavor and a symbolic representation of humanity's relentless quest for exploration. From the elaborative theories posited by Einstein and Rosen to the multidisciplinary contributions by modern physicists engaging with the notion of exotic matter, the historical journey of wormholes illustrates a narrative rich in curiosity, speculation, and interdisciplinary engagement.

This interplay between theory and cultural representation reveals an intricate relationship between the development of scientific understanding and the narratives that shape our collective imagination. Wormholes, whether existing in reality or serving as conceptual bridges in our understanding of the universe, symbolize the crossroads of human aspiration, creativity, and the fundamental quest for knowledge—a quest that spans back through centuries and will continue to echo in the corridors of scientific inquiry. Through this lens, the exploration of wormholes holds a dual significance: it is not merely about navigating the physical cosmos, but also about traversing the terrains of understanding, perception, and the profound mysteries of existence.

2.4. Wormholes Versus Black Holes

A detailed examination of wormholes versus black holes reveals the relationship and distinctions between these two remarkable phenomena that lie at the intersection of theoretical physics and cosmic exploration. Both concepts stem from the foundational principles of general relativity but embody fundamentally different characteristics and implications for our understanding of the universe.

At the essence of the two constructs lies the alteration of spacetime due to mass and energy. Black holes are regions in spacetime where gravity is so intense that nothing—not even light—can escape from them once it crosses a boundary known as the event horizon. The density and gravitational pull of black holes arise when massive stars exhaust their nuclear fuel, causing their cores to undergo gravitational collapse. The resulting singularity manifests a point of infinite density at their center, where the known laws of physics cease to apply. This dramatic end-stage for stars illustrates a transformative fate, one that instills a sense of both fascination and fear regarding the nature of existence.

In sharp contrast, wormholes, often conceptualized as "bridges" through spacetime, provide the potential for traversing distances far beyond the reach of conventional travel. These hypothetical structures could, in theory, shorten the journey between two points in the universe by creating a shortcut through its fabric, thus allowing for faster-than-light travel. Within the framework of general relativity, wormholes stem from solutions to the Einstein Field Equations, most notably the Einstein-Rosen Bridge—the mathematical model linking two points in spacetime. Therefore, while a black hole's nature revolves around its capacity to trap matter and distort spacetime, a wormhole serves as a conduit that might allow movement through the cosmos.

The nature of the two phenomena invites a deeper exploration of their implications. While black holes are characterized by their inherent ability to draw surrounding matter into their depths—often heating it to extreme temperatures and producing X-ray emissions—wormholes demand the existence of exotic matter to stabilize their gravitational structure. This exotic matter would have a negative energy density and serve as a counterbalance to the intense gravitational forces that would collapse a wormhole. The theoretical need for exotic matter heightens the complexity of utilizing wormholes for travel, drawing scientists into a maze of speculation and hypothesis regarding its existence.

The philosophical implications of black holes and wormholes likewise diverge. Black holes pose profound questions about fate, the ultimate end of information, and the nature of singularities. The enigma surrounding what happens to matter when it crosses the event horizon engenders debates on information loss paradoxes, which suggest that information may be irretrievably lost to the universe. This conundrum challenges our understanding of reality and the fabric of existence itself.

Conversely, wormholes beckon inquiries regarding the potential for time travel and interstellar communication. If traversable wormholes could indeed exist, they might permit not only travel across vast distances but possibly also allow for movement through time. This prospect evokes thrilling narratives in science fiction, as characters could jump between different eras, encountering alternate realities or historical events. The discussions surrounding wormholes also lead to broader philosophical ramifications, exploring concepts of causality and the interconnectedness of time and space.

While black holes and wormholes represent two sides of an intriguing cosmic coin, their pursuit within the scientific community has illuminated stark contrasts in both understanding and interpretation. Black holes evoke a sense of caution, emphasizing the perils of the cosmic unknown. They offer a glimpse into the boundaries of current scientific comprehension, prompting efforts to reconcile quantum mechanics with general relativity. Wormholes, however, embody hope and curiosity. They inspire imaginations and provoke adventurous conjectures about travel, exploration, and potential connections between alternate universes.

Given the advancements in scientific inquiry and the allure of both phenomena, researchers remain engaged in ongoing investigations. The fascinating interplay between black holes and wormholes encourages exploration of gravitational waves, spacetime anomalies, and the properties of exotic states of matter, sustaining interest in these cosmic enigmas. As humanity reaches toward the stars, the quest to understand the foundations, implications, and potential of black holes and wormholes remains a testament to our enduring curiosity about the universe and our place within it. In the end, whether one finds intrigue in the terrifying embrace of black holes or the hopeful prospects of wormholes, both concepts serve as gateways to understanding the fabric of reality, eternally shaping our narrative of existence in the cosmos.

2.5. The Einstein-Rosen Bridge

The inquiry into the Einstein-Rosen Bridge, the original conceptualization of wormholes, reveals a sophisticated interplay of mathematics, physics, and philosophy. Proposed by Albert Einstein and Nathan Rosen in their 1935 paper, the bridge was introduced as a theoretical construct to illustrate the potential connections between two distinct points in spacetime, challenging traditional notions of geometry and dimensionality. This model arose from a deeper understanding of general relativity, which dictates how mass and energy influence the curvature of spacetime, creating pathways that may not be immediately visible.

At its essence, the Einstein-Rosen Bridge is a solution to the equations of general relativity that connects two black holes through a tunnel. This bridge structure consists of two openings, known as "mouths," that are connected by a throat, resembling a bridge that spans the gap between two points in the universe. The implications of such a bridge resonate across both theoretical and practical realms, drawing significant attention from physicists and futurists alike. The particular mathematical formulation utilized by Einstein and Rosen elucidates how two black holes could theoretically merge into a single entity, offering access to a different region of spacetime.

To formulate this concept, one must delve into the intricacies of Einstein's field equations, which embody the relationship between the curvature of spacetime and the energy-momentum of whatever occupies that spacetime. The mathematical rigor of the field equations provides a foundation upon which ideas about the Einstein-Rosen Bridge could emerge. Employing a transformation of spherical coordinates to derive the solution, the authors articulated a scenario that allows for the creation of these bridges, illustrating a thought experiment that incites imagination while challenging established scientific frameworks.

One important aspect of the Einstein-Rosen Bridge model is its dimensional properties. The bridge represents a holographic aspect of the universe; it suggests that the universe's entire dimensional makeup can be interconnected in a manner that facilitates travel between distant points. The potential of such interconnectivity raises significant questions regarding the topology of the universe. It introduces the concept of multi-dimensionality and how various dimensions might influence the structure and behavior of spacetime. This pioneering idea led to the philosophical implications regarding reality, suggesting that our understanding of distances and connections may be far from complete.

However, while the Einstein-Rosen Bridge elucidates an intriguing theoretical foundation, it is essential to acknowledge its limitations. Notably, the original model proposed by Einstein and Rosen represents a "non-traversable" wormhole. In essence, it depicts structures that would collapse rapidly upon formation, rendering them unusable for actual travel. This non-traversability stems from the extreme gravitational forces and the event horizons surrounding black holes, which ultimately trap matter and energy, complicating the notion of moving through a bridge.

Despite its conceptual beauty, the Einstein-Rosen Bridge has spurred vibrant debates among theoretical physicists, giving rise to myriad interpretations and extensions of the model. Scholars such as Kip Thorne and others have explored the potential for constructing "traversable" wormholes that might permit travel with the right conditions, particularly emphasizing the necessity of stabilizing exotic matter. This exploration signifies the tension between the abstract theoretical structures and the real-world implications that might allow human traversability.

The conceptual framework of the Einstein-Rosen Bridge also inspires significant discourse in the realms of philosophy and science fiction. As popular culture increasingly employs wormhole themes as a basis for narratives involving time travel, parallel universes, and interstellar adventure, the engagement of audiences widens beyond scientific curiosity to encompass imaginative exploration. The alluring nature of wormhole travel, catalyzed by the postings of Einstein and Rosen, feeds into broader themes of human desire to explore the unknown and transcends both the scientific and philosophical discourses.

As researchers continue to evaluate and expand upon the underlying principles of the Einstein-Rosen Bridge, a compelling array of questions lingers about the very nature of the universe. Could these bridges represent methods of connecting different dimensions, parallel universes, or even provide insights into the cosmos's fundamental fabric? What roles do exotic matter, quantum fluctuations, and advanced technology play in the feasibility of traversing a wormhole? As these questions guide inquiry, the legacy of the Einstein-Rosen Bridge remains integral to the exploration of wormhole travel, inspiring both scientific rigor in academic circles and imaginative whimsy in the hearts and minds of those gazing upwards toward the stars.

In summary, the Einstein-Rosen Bridge embodies a profound intersection of theoretical physics and philosophical inquiry. It invites us to reconsider the boundaries of our knowledge about spacetime, pushing beyond conventional limits while simultaneously igniting our capacity for imagination. The bridge serves not only as a mathematical model but also as a symbol of our relentless pursuit of discovery, fostering curiosity about the grand cosmos and our aspiration to traverse its enigmatic vastness. Thus, as dialogues about wormholes continue to emerge, the echoes of Einstein and Rosen's groundbreaking work will resonate, inviting future generations of thinkers, dreamers, and explorers to fathom the depths of the universe —one bridged connection at a time.

3. Theoretical Foundations of Wormhole Science

3.1. General Relativity and Spacetime

The exploration of Einstein's theory of General Relativity is foundational to understanding the concept of wormholes, which represent intriguing theoretical constructs emerging from the complex interplay between mass, energy, and the fabric of spacetime. General relativity, formulated by Albert Einstein in 1915, posits that the force we perceive as gravity is not a traditional force but rather the result of spacetime curvature caused by the presence of mass and energy. This groundbreaking idea reshaped our understanding of the cosmos, allowing for a deeper comprehension of how light travels, how celestial bodies interact, and how time itself can be influenced by gravitational fields.

At its core, general relativity places forth the notion that spacetime is a four-dimensional continuum, where the three dimensions of space are fused with the dimension of time. This innovative approach led to the revolutionary insight that objects with mass cause the fabric of spacetime to warp, creating what we perceive as gravity. Imagine a heavy ball placed in the center of a stretched rubber sheet; the ball causes the sheet to sag around it, illustrating how larger masses distort spacetime and how smaller objects move along the curves created by this distortion.

Within this framework, the concept of wormholes emerges as a fascinating potentiality. Following the theoretical groundwork laid by Einstein and his colleague Nathan Rosen, wormholes are posited as tunnels or bridges connecting two separate points in the universe, allowing for instantaneous travel between distant locations. The idea of a wormhole captures the imagination, suggesting a means to transcend the limits of light speed and the immense distances of interstellar travel. However, these tunnels also invite serious scientific inquiry, pushing us to consider the nature of spacetime itself and the implications that arise from manipulating it.

When examining wormholes through the lens of general relativity, the Einstein-Rosen Bridge serves as a pivotal concept. This theoretical structure describes a pair of black holes linked by a tunnel, essentially proposing that two distant regions of spacetime could be interconnected in ways that allow for travel between them. The initial model, while mathematically elegant, reveals significant challenges, particularly concerning the stability and traversability of such structures. The original form of the Einstein-Rosen Bridge, as proposed by its creators, is non-traversable, meaning that it appears to be fundamentally unsuitable for actual travel due to its rapid collapse upon formation. This limitation fuels ongoing theoretical explorations, as scientists endeavor to identify conditions that might allow for traversable wormholes that could accommodate human travel.

The mathematical underpinnings of general relativity introduce complexities that challenge our understanding of traditional physics. Within the Einstein Field Equations—a set of ten interrelated differential equations—lies the relationship between the curvature of spacetime and the energy-momentum tensor, which represents the distribution of mass and energy. Solutions to these equations can lead to distinct outcomes, some of which, like the Schwarzschild solution, describe gravitational fields around non-rotating black holes, while others provide insights into the structure and nature of wormholes. The exploration of these solutions illustrates the rich terrain that intertwines spacetime geometry, black holes, and potential wormhole architectures.

Crucially, the exploration of wormholes through the prism of general relativity introduces the concept of "exotic matter," hypothesized substances with negative energy density essential for maintaining the stability of a traversable wormhole. Negative energy scenarios become critical in ensuring that the gravitational collapse does not obliterate the wormhole structure. In essence, exotic matter would counteract the intense gravitational forces at play, creating a stable condition necessary for traversal. However, the existence of such matter remains hypothetical and invites further exploration within the realms of quantum mechanics and theoretical physics.

As advances are made in understanding the implications of general relativity, the intersection with quantum mechanics further complicates the discourse. Quantum fluctuations may lead to the spontaneous formation of micro-wormholes on extraordinarily tiny scales, prompting exciting questions about the possible connections they might suggest between quantum gravity and cosmological phenomena. The dual frameworks of general relativity and quantum mechanics wrestle with the complexities of reality, leading to broader inquiries into the nature of spacetime and how we might manipulate it.

The implications of wormholes extend beyond empirical science, prompting deep philosophical considerations regarding time, reality, and existence itself. If wormholes could indeed serve as portals through spacetime, the very concept of linear time as we understand it would be called into question. Time travel, enabled by traversable wormholes, presents paradoxes and conundrums that stretch the limits of our philosophical frameworks, challenging our perceptions of causality and free will.

Moreover, within the realm of popular culture, the notion of wormholes has fueled creative narratives that resonate with humanity's enduring thirst for exploration and adventure. Films, literature, and other forms of media have embraced wormholes as symbols of escapism and the quest for understanding the unknown, giving life to speculative journeys that marry science with imagination.

In summary, the exploration of general relativity and its implications for wormhole science presents a complex and rich tapestry of inquiry. The interactions between mass, energy, and the curvature of spacetime give rise to profound questions and possibilities, challenging our perceptions and inviting us to rethink our understanding of the universe. As scientists continue to unravel the intricacies of these cosmic structures, the journey into the heart of wormholes remains a testament to the power of curiosity, sparking a dialogue that intertwines scientific rigor with philosophical wonder, and propelling the quest for knowledge forward into the infinite.

3.2. Quantum Mechanics and Their Role

The intersection of quantum mechanics and wormhole theory reveals a realm of fascinating possibilities, where the very fabric of spacetime is intertwined with the principles of quantum physics. The quantum world behaves in ways that often defy our conventional understanding, and it opens avenues for far-reaching implications regarding phenomena such as wormholes, time travel, and the nature of reality.

Quantum mechanics, the branch of physics that deals with the behavior of particles at the smallest scales, introduces concepts such as superposition, entanglement, and uncertainty. These principles challenge our classical intuitions, suggesting that particles can exist in multiple states at once, can instantaneously affect each other across vast distances, and that the outcome of certain measurements cannot be predicted with certainty. This curious nature of particles is critical when we consider the implications for wormhole travel, as it posits scenarios wherein spacetime itself might behave differently than we traditionally conceive.

One of the most intriguing aspects of quantum mechanics relates to its suggestion of closed timelike curves, paths in spacetime that loop back on themselves, potentially allowing for time travel. If such curves exist, they may be represented mathematically through the fabric of a traversable wormhole. The implications of this theory are profound, as they introduce the possibility not merely of traveling vast distances through space, but also of navigating through time. For instance, if one could enter a wormhole at a designated point, they might emerge not only at a different location in space but at a different moment in time. Herein lies a tantalizing paradox: can we rewrite history or perhaps even interact with our own past selves? This concept is fraught with philosophical implications regarding causality and the flow of time itself.

The role of quantum fluctuations also plays a significant part in the discourse surrounding wormholes. According to quantum mechanics, vacuum states are never truly empty; they are teeming with transient particles that pop in and out of existence. Some theoretical physicists postulate that, on infinitesimally small scales, these fluctuations could result in the spontaneous formation of micro-wormholes— tiny, ephemeral connections between different points in spacetime. Although these micro-wormholes would be too minuscule to traverse with conventional technology, they hint at the possibility that the universe itself might harbor these tunnels in its underlying structure. Such insights inspire curiosity about whether these ephemeral structures could lead to significant discoveries regarding the fundamental nature of the cosmos.

Furthermore, the interrelationship between quantum mechanics and general relativity—two pillars of modern physics—has long been a source of debate and inquiry. While general relativity excels at describing the behavior of massive objects and the structure of spacetime, quantum mechanics provides valuable insights into the subatomic realm. However, reconciling these two frameworks has remained a challenge, often labeled as the quest for a theory of quantum gravity. This endeavor is essential in any exploration of wormholes, as achieving a unified understanding could illuminate the properties of these theoretical structures and reveal whether they can exist in our universe. Scientists like Stephen Hawking and Kip Thorne have contemplated various models, seeking to understand the compatibility of quantum mechanics with general relativity and the circumstances under which traversable wormholes may operate.

A significant aspect of this inquiry pertains to exotic matter, a hypothetical substance that would need to possess negative energy density to allow stable wormholes to exist without collapsing. Quantum theories anticipate that certain configurations of energy could lead to scenarios where exotic matter could be realized, prompting speculation about its potential presence in the universe. As physicists delve deeper into the quantum makeup of reality, finding or creating exotic matter could become a linchpin in framing discussions about the actual feasibility of wormhole travel.

The philosophical ramifications of aligning quantum mechanics with wormhole theory further enrich the conversation. These explorations push us to grapple with questions about reality, individuality, and the fundamental nature of existence—questions that have long intrigued humanity. Does the very existence of wormholes mean that our perception of time and causality is limited? If time is not linear, what does that imply for human experience and agency? If one could travel through a wormhole and potentially alter past events, how might our understanding of responsibility and ethics change?

The fusion of quantum mechanics with wormhole science ultimately invites a resolve to bridge disciplinary boundaries, forging connections between physics, philosophy, and science fiction. By embracing both the empirical rigor of quantum theories and the imaginative possibilities inherent in wormhole construction and traversal, researchers open up new frontiers that invigorate the scientific discourse on these cosmic enigmas.

In summary, the role of quantum mechanics in the study of wormholes transcends mere speculation; it elicits profound questions regarding time, causality, and the nature of reality. The interplay between theoretical constructs and philosophical inquiries provides a fertile ground for exploration, challenging us to reimagine our relationship with the universe. As our understanding of these complex concepts deepens, we embark on a quest that may redefine the meanings of space and time, paving the way for potential discoveries that lie beyond the traditional confines of our understanding. The journey into the realm of wormholes and quantum mechanics is as much about scientific exploration as it is about harnessing the power of imagination—a testament to humanity's unquenchable curiosity and relentless pursuit of the unknown.

3.3. Exotic Matter Requirement

In the fascinating realm of theoretical physics, the concept of wormholes leads us to one crucial element that underpins their potential existence and traversability: exotic matter. For a wormhole to function as a stable conduit through spacetime, it requires specific characteristics of matter that challenge our conventional understanding of physics. This exotic matter is defined by its unique property of negative energy density, which distinguishes it from the matter we encounter in our everyday lives, which inherently carries positive energy density.

To begin to grasp the significance of exotic matter in sustaining a wormhole, we must first understand the basic structure of a wormhole as theorized in the framework of general relativity. A classic depiction of a wormhole is that of a tunnel connecting two mouths, separated by a throat that acts as the passage between different regions of spacetime. In the absence of exotic matter, the immense gravitational forces surrounding a wormhole's throat would cause it to collapse almost instantaneously under normal circumstances. This collapse occurs due to the tremendous energies associated with gravitational attraction, which would compress the structure and obliterate any chance of traversing through it.

It is in this context that exotic matter plays a pivotal role. For a traversable wormhole to remain open, the gravitational influences must be counterbalanced to avoid collapse. Here, exotic matter steps in— hypothetically possessing properties that allow it to exert a repulsive gravitational force. Unlike normal matter, which increases its gravitational pull alongside its accumulation, exotic matter would exhibit behavior contrary to this trend, enabling it to stabilize the wormhole's throat. By providing a sort of cushion against gravitational forces, exotic matter would allow the passage through the wormhole to persist over time, theoretically enabling a journey through its curvilinear structure.

The notion of exotic matter is deeply rooted in theoretical physics, and researchers have highlighted various potential forms and sources of such matter. One possibility hypothesized stems from the principles of quantum field theory, wherein the energy fluctuates around vacuum states. This principle of fluctuation could produce conditions where negative energy density arises temporarily, albeit on a microscopic scale. Some scientists have proposed that this micro-exotic matter could potentially be harnessed or manipulated, albeit the practicalities of achieving this remain speculative and largely theoretical.

Another avenue of exploration regarding the existence of exotic matter lies within the context of Casimir effects, which arise from the quantum field theory. The Casimir effect describes the attractive force that occurs between two uncharged, parallel conducting plates placed in a vacuum. The vacuum between the plates is devoid of the normal positive energy pressure waves, leading to a diminishment of energy density relative to the surrounding space, which could be exploited to generate local regions of negative energy density. The implications of harnessing such effects would be monumental, positioning exotic matter as a tangible entity that may support the formation of wormholes.

While exotic matter remains a theoretical construct, the implications of attempting to manifest or discover it extend far beyond mere scientific curiosity. If it were possible to find or create exotic matter, the very fabric of our understanding of physics and the universe could shift dramatically, opening new pathways for space exploration, advanced technologies, and even hinting at the existence of more intricate structures and dimensions beyond our current understanding.

However, the exploration of exotic matter invites complex inquiries. Several questions arise regarding the intrinsic properties of this matter: How would it interact with regular matter? What would its stability be under varying conditions? How could we conceive of it existing in sufficient quantities to stabilize an actual wormhole?

These queries underline the scientific debates that surround the viability of wormholes as potential portals for traversing across the vast cosmic landscape. The ethereal properties attributed to exotic matter leave us straddling the boundary between established physics and realms of speculative inquiry. The quest for exotic matter remains a testament to our unwavering human endeavor to push boundaries, unravel mysteries, and explore the unknown realms of the universe.

In conclusion, the requirement of exotic matter represents not merely a technical detail in the theoretical construction of wormholes, but a profound challenge that propels forward our understanding of gravity, spacetime, and the limits of our known universe. As research continues and technology advances, the investigation into exotic matter and its application in wormhole science could yield transformative findings, potentially rewriting the narrative of human space exploration and the very nature of reality itself. The implications are vast, inviting both rigorous scientific inquiry and visionary speculation as we contemplate the tantalizing prospects of traversable wormholes that could one day bridge the immense distances of the cosmos.

3.4. Famous Physicists' Contributions

In the intricate web of theoretical physics, certain names resonate deeply with the community as pioneers in the study of wormholes and their fascinating implications for our understanding of the universe. Among these luminaries, Kip Thorne stands out, not solely for his contributions to gravitational physics, but also for his role in translating complex scientific concepts into accessible narratives. Thorne's work in the realm of wormholes, particularly his research on traversable wormholes, has significantly shaped both the scientific discourse and popular imagination surrounding these enigmatic structures.

Kip Thorne's influence in the field began as he delved into the possibilities afforded by general relativity. His groundbreaking contribution came in the late 20th century when he, alongside collaborative efforts with other physicists, exemplified how traversable wormholes could potentially be maintained using exotic matter. In his seminal paper on this topic published in 1988, Thorne outlined the theoretical framework necessary for creating a stable wormhole capable of human travel. He meticulously established the conditions under which such wormholes might exist, emphasizing the role of negative energy density—an idea that would become critical in discussions about the feasibility of actual wormhole travel.

Furthermore, Thorne's work extended beyond theoretical frameworks; he actively engaged with the speculative implications of his research. His vision spanned both scientific inquiry and cultural commentary, particularly exemplified through his involvement in the creation of the film "Interstellar." Drawing on his own scientific principles, Thorne contributed to the screenplay and consulted on the portrayal of black holes and wormholes, bringing a sense of realism to the film's narrative. Through fiction, he bridged the gap between complex physics and public engagement, stirring interest and curiosity about astrophysical phenomena.

Alongside Thorne, pioneers like John Archibald Wheeler played pivotal roles in the evolution of wormhole concepts. Wheeler's coining of the term "wormhole" itself symbolizes the powerful blend of imagination and scientific rigor that characterizes the exploration of these cosmic structures. Wheeler's contributions to the discourse on spacetime topology and quantum gravity laid foundational groundwork for further explorations into the nature of wormholes, as he posed questions that echoed through decades of scientific inquiry.

Another critical figure, Stephen Hawking, while primarily recognized for his work on black holes, also touched upon themes relevant to wormhole theory. Hawking's insights into the nature of singularities and the behaviors of particles within intense gravitational fields indirectly influenced the discussions surrounding wormholes. His inquiries into the fabric of spacetime prompted new understandings of how the universe might be interconnected, further accentuating the potential implications of wormhole theory.

The contributions of these physicists formed a robust framework for the ongoing exploration of wormholes, each adding unique perspectives that propelled the field forward. Their research and dialogues collectively crystallized the understanding that wormholes, while still situated in the realm of speculation, possess a rich mathematical and theoretical foundation rooted in the principles of general relativity and quantum mechanics.

Beyond the realms of established scientists, the discourse surrounding wormholes has compelled the involvement of interdisciplinary thinkers, policymakers, and cultural influencers, each contributing to the dialogues surrounding the implications of such constructs. The collaboration across borders of discipline underscores the potency of the idea of wormholes to captivate the human imagination, transcending the confines of academia to permeate popular culture.

Notably, the interest in wormholes reverberates in the feedback loop between scientific research and its cultural representations. As physics continues to probe the potential existence and properties of wormholes, the speculative nature of wormhole travel invites an ongoing exploration of its narratives within literature, film, and art. The dynamic interplay between the scientific community's pursuit of knowledge and the creative expressions that arise from it symbolizes humanity's enduring quest to understand our place in the universe.

As we reflect on these contributions, it becomes evident that the pursuit of comprehension regarding wormholes does not reside solely within the confines of theoretical physics. It encapsulates a broader narrative about exploration, curiosity, and the interlacing of science and imagination. The vibrant tapestry woven by the efforts of physicists such as Thorne, Wheeler, and Hawking continues to inspire new generations of scientists and dreamers alike. The exploration of wormholes challenges us to contemplate the limits of our understanding, urging us to look beyond the known and push the boundaries of what might one day be achievable. Each stride made in unraveling the complexities of wormholes not only enriches our scientific landscape but also reminds us of the infinite possibilities that await in the cosmic expanse.

3.5. The Fluctuation of Spacetime

In the realm of theoretical physics, the notion of spacetime fluctuations paves the way for the intriguing concept of micro-wormholes —tiny, ephemeral connections that may occur within the fabric of the universe on scales that defy our traditional understanding. These fluctuations arise from the inherent unpredictability of quantum mechanics, suggesting that the fabric of spacetime is not static but rather constantly shifting and dynamic. Such transient wormholes might not only illuminate the potential for connecting distant regions of the cosmos but also provide insight into the very nature of reality itself.

At the quantum level, the universe is filled with energy fluctuations, and it is within these lively dynamics that wormholes might emerge, albeit momentarily. According to theories, the vacuum of space is not empty; instead, it is replete with fleeting virtual particles that materialize and annihilate in the blink of an eye. This phenomenon, termed quantum foam, implies a bubbling chaotic state where spacetime can twist, bend, and form short-lived bridges at the smallest scales. The existence of micro-wormholes could represent a direct consequence of this foamy spacetime, implying that in some ways, the universe may harbor a vast network of these minuscule structures.

The theoretical underpinnings to these micro-wormholes spring from a combination of quantum field theory and gravitation, whereby the interplay between energy states generates conditions that permit such phenomena to occur. Notably, the concept of quantum tunneling provides a compelling analogy; particles possess a probability of transcending barriers they typically cannot surmount, similarly suggesting that spacetime itself may permit tunneling through wormholes under specific conditions. The potential for micro-wormholes to exist naturally suggests that spacetime is far more intricate than previously assumed, laying the groundwork for novel possibilities regarding travel and connection in the universe.

However, the implications of naturally occurring micro-wormholes extend beyond mere curiosity and into profound philosophical considerations. If these micro-wormholes exist, they might hint at a fundamentally interconnected universe where locations and events are not isolated but rather woven into a vast tapestry of possibilities. This interconnectivity invites speculation about the nature of reality: if microscopic bridges can spontaneously connect distant points in spacetime, what does this imply for our understanding of distance, time, and potentially even causality?

Moreover, the investigation into micro-wormholes holds tantalizing implications for the broader study of wormholes at a macroscopic scale. Understanding how these structures form could inform theories on constructing stable, traversable wormholes for potential space travel. While our current technological capabilities may not allow us to directly engage with or observe these micro-wormholes, the theoretical exploration of their origins and properties can inspire innovative approaches and methods to search for evidence of these phenomena in the cosmos.

Scientific discourse surrounding micro-wormholes reinforces the notion that our understanding of the universe is still in its infancy. As physicists endeavor to unravel the mysteries of quantum fluctuations, they simultaneously rush to bridge the gap between quantum mechanics and general relativity—a pursuit fraught with challenges but rich in potential. Each revelation regarding the existence and behavior of micro-wormholes may open doors to further inquiries into broader theories of spacetime geometry and its implications for our universe.

In summary, the fluctuation of spacetime and the potential emergence of micro-wormholes represent not just theoretical musings; they encapsulate the heart of astrophysical inquiry, urging us to challenge existing paradigms and consider the universe's vastness, intricacy, and wonder. The exploration of these ephemeral structures catalyzes a rethinking of our relationship with spacetime, compelling us to journey deeper into the mysteries of the cosmos. As we continue to unravel the complexities of quantum phenomena, we may find ourselves closer to understanding the profound implications these tiny wormholes hold for our perceptions of connection, travel, and existence itself, ultimately reshaping our narrative of the universe as a fluid, interwoven expanse just waiting to be explored.

4. Scientific Debates and Controversies

4.1. The Possibility of Traversability

Exploring the possibility of traversability through wormholes is a complex and multifaceted discussion that intertwines theoretical physics, cosmology, and speculative technology. The concept of traversing a wormhole presupposes that these mysterious constructs exist not just as theoretical constructs, but as practical pathways that could enable movement across vast distances in space and potentially through time. This proposition evokes both excitement and skepticism in the scientific community, as the reliability of wormhole travel hinges on a myriad of scientific understandings and assumptions.

At the heart of any discussion on traversable wormholes is the imbalance of gravitational forces and the necessity for exotic matter. A traversable wormhole is theorized to consist of two openings, or "mouths," separated by a curved throat through spacetime. For a wormhole to remain stable and open long enough for matter—say, a spacecraft or a human—to traverse safely, the throat would need to be kept open against the immense gravitational pressure attempting to close it. It is here where exotic matter, hypothesized to have negative energy density, comes into play. Such matter would counteract the compressive forces, allowing a stable passage that does not collapse the structure under ordinary conditions.

The challenge arises, however, because the existence of exotic matter itself remains speculative. Although certain theories within quantum physics suggest its potential, empirical evidence for exotic matter has yet to be observed. If exotic matter truly exists and can be harnessed, scientists theorize that a sufficiently advanced civilization could construct or stabilize a wormhole, making traversability a tangible possibility. Conversely, if exotic matter cannot exist or be synthesized in sufficient quantities, the dream of traversing wormholes may remain just that—a dream.

Another layer to consider is the nature of spacetime itself. Modern physics posits that spacetime is not a fixed backdrop but a dynamic entity that can be deformed and stretched, enabling the conceptualization of wormholes. Theoretical physicists use mathematical models to explore various configurations of wormholes, each with distinct properties and implications for traversability. For example, the Einstein-Rosen Bridge initially proposed by Albert Einstein and Nathan Rosen illustrates a non-traversable wormhole that collapses upon formation, raising questions about how to create a wormhole that one could actually enter and exit without being annihilated.

Additionally, discussions of traversability lead to critical questions about the effects of time dilation and causality. If wormholes could permit travel across vast distances in minimal time, the implications for time travel are staggering. The passage from one end of a wormhole to another might enable one to emerge not just at a different spatial location, but at a different temporal coordinate. This revelation introduces paradoxes, such as the grandfather paradox—what happens if one travels back in time and inadvertently prevents their grandfather from meeting their grandmother, thereby negating their own existence? Scholars struggle with reconciling these ideas of causality with the remnants of quantum mechanics, which suggest that alternate histories and timelines might coexist in a multiversal tapestry.

The practicality of traversing a wormhole also brings forth rigorous considerations regarding the technologies required for such journeys. Would it be feasible to construct a spacecraft capable of navigating through a wormhole? What protections would be necessary to shield occupants from potential radiation or extreme gravitational tides? Theoretical designs explore these possibilities, but tangible technological advancements remain grounded more in science fiction than in present reality.

Despite the vast unknowns surrounding wormholes and their traversability, the scientific pursuit is filled with optimism. As research continues into theoretical models, quantum developments, and the potential for exotic matter, the scientific community remains unwavering in its exploration of these cosmic constructs. The exploration of wormholes embodies humanity's relentless pursuit of knowledge and its desire to stretch the paradigms of previously established scientific boundaries.

This possibility of traversability ultimately serves as both a scientific challenge and an imaginative frontier. Beyond the calculations and technical theories lie profound philosophical inquiries about our relationship to space, time, and reality itself. The image of stepping through a wormhole, bridging unimaginable distances, tantalizes the human spirit, representing not only the hope for deep space exploration but also a profound yearning to understand the universe and our place within it.

As we venture further into the realms of theoretical physics, the discourse surrounding the possibility of traversing wormholes promises to ignite wonder and curiosity for generations to come. Each stride made toward understanding these complex structures fuels the imagination and instigates the quest toward uncovering the mysteries that dwell within the cosmos, always drawing us closer to the intriguing prospect of stepping through the cosmic doorway that wormholes represent. Whether or not traversable wormholes exist will depend largely on the continued evolution of our scientific understanding, the technological innovations of tomorrow, and perhaps even our ability to reconcile the philosophical implications of a universe rich with possibilities.

4.2. The Paradox of Time Travel

The complexities surrounding time travel through wormholes introduce a plethora of fascinating paradoxes that resonate deeply within both scientific and philosophical realms. As we delve into the paradox of time travel, it becomes essential to dissect the intricate relationships between causality, temporal continuity, and the very nature of existence itself.

At the core of the time travel paradoxes lies the concept of causality —the principle that each effect has a preceding cause. When we introduce wormholes into this framework, particularly those that could enable travel back in time, we confront scenarios that challenge conventional understanding. The classic illustration is the grandfather paradox: what would happen if one were to travel back in time and inadvertently prevent their grandfather from meeting their grandmother? The result of such an action would be a logical inconsistency, where the time traveler could never have existed to travel back in the first place. This contradiction raises profound questions about the fabric of reality and whether time can be revisited or altered.

The theoretical implications of wormholes suggest that they could create paths in spacetime where the rules of causality may not strictly apply. Some physicists propose scenarios where timelines could branch into parallel universes, allowing for alternative outcomes. In this multiverse model, if a time traveler were to change something in the past, they would not alter their original timeline but rather create a new branch that diverges from it. This notion alleviates the paradoxical tension by suggesting that every decision could spawn separate realities, each existing concurrently within an expansive multiverse. Still, the idea of parallel universes poses its own set of philosophical inquiries about identity, fate, and the interconnectedness of choices.

Moreover, the implications of traveling through a wormhole to a past moment ripple through our understanding of time itself. Time, traditionally perceived as linear—flowing in one direction from past to present to future—comes into question when we consider the spatial shortcuts that wormholes may provide. If time is not a fixed progression but rather a malleable framework where moments can be accessed non-sequentially, then our existential understanding of before and after is fundamentally disrupted. Would we then consider time to be a mere construct, an illusion upheld by human perception, while the universe fundamentally exists within a timeless state?

The considerations surrounding time travel also grapple with the philosophical debates of free will versus determinism. If one accepts that the past can be altered, questions arise regarding the autonomy of decisions and the implications for moral responsibility. In a scenario where individuals can travel back to modify past actions, does this imply that choices are predetermined, or can one genuinely exercise free will in shaping their history? These inquiries instigate discussions about the ethics surrounding time travel, as the ability to influence events brings about moral dilemmas regarding consequences and accountability.

Furthermore, the potential for time travel through wormholes invites reconsideration of identity over time. If one were to step into a wormhole and emerge in the past, how do we perceive the continuity of the self? Philosophers contemplate whether a person retains their identity through fluctuations in temporal existence or whether interactions with alternate timelines create divergences in personal identity. The exploration of this question can lead to cognitive dissonance regarding how our life stories and personal narratives intertwine with the linear perception of time.

Finally, the paradox of time travel must confront the constraints imposed by physical laws and theories. General relativity accommodates the idea of closed timelike curves, which can theoretically permit backward time travel through specific conditions, yet these scenarios often evoke skepticism. The energy requirements, the role of exotic matter, and the unresolved challenges of maintaining stable wormholes introduce significant barriers that may render such travel practically unattainable. Thus, while the theoretical framework allows for rich discussions about the implications of time travel, practical realizations remain imbued with uncertainty.

In conclusion, the paradox of time travel through wormholes envelops a web of scientific, philosophical, and ethical conundrums. From causality to identity, each thread invites inquiry and challenges our understanding of reality's very foundation. As we navigate through the complexities of time, our exploration illuminates profound reflections on existence, urging us to consider the parameters that shape our perception and understanding of the cosmos. The journey into the enigma of time travel not only serves to expand the horizons of theoretical physics but also enriches our philosophical discourse, creating a dialogue that positions humanity at the fulcrum of time's intricate dance.

4.3. Stability and Collapse Issues

The stability and collapse issues associated with wormhole constructs present intricate challenges that scientists must grapple with in their theoretical explorations of these cosmic bridges. While the notion of traversing vast distances or potentially navigating through time via wormholes captivates the imagination, the fundamental question of whether these structures could genuinely exist and remain traversable under realistic conditions warrants serious scrutiny.

At the heart of the stability issues lies the requirement for exotic matter. As previously discussed, a traversable wormhole would consist of two mouths connected by a throat. The intense gravitational forces at play in these structures pose an inherent risk: without some form of counterbalancing force, a wormhole is likely to collapse almost instantaneously upon formation. The gravitational pressure from standard matter would compress the throat, effectively sealing it off and eliminating any potential for travel. This vulnerability underscores the importance of exotic matter possessing negative energy density, which can counteract or negate the collapsive gravitational forces. Researchers theorize that such exotic matter would form a sort of stabilizing "shell" around the throat, allowing a wormhole to persist long enough for traversal.

However, the actual existence of exotic matter remains an open question in the scientific community. While theories suggest potential sources of such matter, including quantum fluctuations and Casimir effects, empirical evidence is sadly lacking. This uncertainty invites skepticism about whether traversable wormholes can be built in a physically realistic universe, and if they can be, whether our understanding of the properties of exotic matter is sufficiently developed to engineer them without collapse.

Another element contributing to the stability issue pertains to the geometry of spacetime itself. The dynamic interplay of spacetime curvature influenced by mass and energy is a cornerstone of general relativity, and it introduces complexities for the theoretical underpinnings of wormholes. Certain configurations of wormholes, particularly those arising from simplistic models, may not sufficiently account for the curved nature of spacetime, resulting in unstable structures prone to collapse. The mathematical models that physicists employ to describe wormholes often engage complex metrics that map the shape and behavior of the wormhole within spacetime. If these metrics are not accurately represented, the validity of any conclusions drawn about a wormhole's stability is inherently compromised.

Furthermore, external cosmic influences cannot be overlooked. The environment surrounding a wormhole, dominated by other gravitational bodies, may exert forces that destabilize the delicate balance required for a stable wormhole formation. For instance, if a wormhole were situated within a region of active astrophysical phenomena —planetary formations, radiation fields, or gravitational waves—the fluctuating conditions could introduce perturbations that challenge the stability of the wormhole's throat. The cosmic dance of celestial bodies introduces variables that might not be fully accounted for in current theoretical frameworks.

The role of Hawking radiation also interjects complications into the dialogue surrounding wormhole stability. Stephen Hawking, through his groundbreaking work, introduced the concept of black hole evaporation via Hawking radiation, where black holes could lose mass over time through the radiation of thermal energy. If wormholes share properties with black holes, the same mechanism could spell doom for them. A traversable wormhole could theoretically lose stability as it leaked energy, leading to a collapse of its structure. Understanding how Hawking radiation would affect a wormhole remains an ongoing area of research, as physicists explore the implications of this radiation on the potential lifespan and utility of traversable wormholes.

In sum, the exploration of stability and collapse issues surrounding wormholes encompasses multifaceted inquiries, threading together theoretical concerns, potential technological hurdles, and cosmic considerations. The quest to comprehend what might prevent a wormhole from collapsing invokes a careful balancing act among gravitational forces, exotic matter, spacetime geometry, and cosmic influences. The dialogue surrounding these challenges serves to underscore the complexities of advancing our understanding of wormholes—not merely as mathematical constructs, but as potential realities intertwined with the nature of our universe.

As scientists continue to probe the depths of these issues, they also foment discussions about broader implications. What would successful traversal through a stable wormhole mean for our understanding of the universe? How would it redefine our concepts of distance and time? These reflections encourage an ongoing exploration of the cosmos, prompting both theoretical inquiries and imaginative narratives about humanity's potential engagement with these extraordinary entities that straddle the boundaries of science and speculation. With each new insight, the notion of wormholes continues to inspire, inviting further exploration into the profound mysteries of existence that lie just beyond the horizon of our understanding.

4.4. The Role of Hawking Radiation

In the fascinating realm of theoretical physics, the role of Hawking radiation plays an intriguing and complex part in the discussion surrounding the stability and integrity of wormholes. Stephen Hawking's groundbreaking work on black holes introduced the concept of Hawking radiation, positing that black holes are not completely black but emit radiation due to quantum effects near the event horizon. This radiation suggests that black holes can lose mass over time, ultimately leading to their evaporation. When we consider the implications of this phenomenon for wormholes, it becomes clear that understanding Hawking radiation is crucial to assessing the practicality of traversable wormholes.

The foundational principle of Hawking radiation derives from the application of quantum mechanics in curved spacetime—the very context in which wormholes are theorized to exist. Hawking proposed that particle-antiparticle pairs spontaneously formed near the event horizon of black holes can lead to one particle falling into the black hole while the other escapes, leading to a measurable radiation effect. In essence, this radiation serves as a mechanism through which black holes could lose energy and mass, eventually resulting in their potential disappearance.

When applied to the context of wormholes, the concept of Hawking radiation raises significant questions regarding their stability. If a wormhole possesses characteristics similar to those of black holes, it might face similar challenges regarding its longevity and integrity. For a traversable wormhole to be functional, it must remain stable over time, allowing for safe passage between its two mouths. However, if such wormholes were susceptible to Hawking radiation or mechanisms akin to the evaporation observed in black holes, it could lead to a rapid loss of structural integrity, causing them to collapse before anyone could traverse them.

The dynamic interplay of quantum fluctuations and spacetime curvature suggests that some form of Hawking-like radiation might also emanate from wormholes, impacting their maintenance and performance. As a wormhole engulfs exotic matter or experiences gravitational influences, it might encounter similar radiation patterns that could jeopardize its stability. Theoretically, if a wormhole were to lose too much energy too quickly, it could lead to its eventual closure, proving it to be non-traversable for practical travel. Therefore, understanding the potential emissions of Hawking radiation or their equivalence in the context of traversable wormholes becomes crucial for assessing the viability of such cosmic constructs.

Further complicating matters, the implications of Hawking radiation extend into the discussions surrounding information loss paradoxes and the nature of reality itself. As several interpretations have arisen from the implications of black hole evaporation, including questions about where the information contained within that matter goes once the black hole evaporates, similar inquiries emerge regarding wormholes. If one were to traverse a wormhole, could the information, or the very essence of a traveler, be irretrievably lost? The uncertainty surrounding whether this information would be preserved complicates not only the theoretical framework of wormholes but also our understanding of reality and existence itself.

Additionally, the exploration of Hawking radiation invites newer avenues of research into the potential connections between black holes and wormholes. Some theorists speculate on the nature of black holes as gateway structures, implying that the radiation emitted can somehow connect to the stable or unstable mechanisms of wormholes. This line of exploration opens up avenues to consider whether traversing black holes might also lead to traversable wormholes in some theoretical framework, transforming our conception of celestial navigation and the architectures of the universe.

In summary, the role of Hawking radiation in relation to wormholes epitomizes the intricate interplay between quantum mechanics, general relativity, and gravitation. Hawking's theories on black holes illuminate critical considerations for the stability and practicality of wormholes as potential conduits through spacetime. The challenges introduced by radiation emissions and energy loss necessitate a deeper understanding of both phenomena, compelling scientists to grapple with tantalizing questions of information, reality, and stability that lie at the heart of wormhole exploration. As research continues in these domains, the complex relationship between Hawking radiation and traversable wormholes underscores humanity's persistent quest to understand the formidable mysteries embedded within the cosmos, propelling us further into the unknown possibilities awaiting our discovery.

4.5. The Cosmic Censorship Conjecture

The Cosmic Censorship Conjecture is a captivating theoretical framework proposed to address the possible existence of naked singularities within the universe. This conjecture essentially posits that the fundamental laws of general relativity would prevent singularities—regions where spacetime curvature becomes infinite and the known laws of physics fail—from being visible to distant observers. In essence, the conjecture suggests that singularities formed within the context of gravitational collapse, such as those found at the center of black holes, must always be cloaked by an event horizon, which acts as a one-way membrane, sealing off the singularity from the rest of the universe.

The implications of this conjecture are far-reaching, influencing the understanding of black holes, the nature of spacetime, and the fundamental structure of the universe. If we accept the validity of the cosmic censorship conjecture, it leads to the assertion that event horizons inherently protect observers from the paradoxes and complexities associated with singularities. On the other hand, should naked singularities exist, they would challenge core tenets of physics, revealing potentially observable phenomena that could alter the relationship between matter, light, and spacetime itself.

To grasp the significance of the cosmic censorship conjecture, it is necessary to delve into the mathematical foundations laid by general relativity. In the realm of relativistic physics, singularities emerge as mathematical entities that arise in certain solutions of the Einstein Field Equations, representing conditions under which material points converge to infinite density. These singularities, manifested in theoretical discussions surrounding black holes, challenge the completeness of the theory because they create scenarios where predictions break down, leading to ambiguities in causality and the behavior of particles and fields in their vicinity.

The theory of black hole formation, according to general relativity, suggests that upon the gravitational collapse of a massive star, the core may culminate in a singularity enclosed within an event horizon —commonly regarded as the point of no return. The event horizon establishes a boundary beyond which information cannot escape; thus, it ensures that the singularity remains hidden from external observers. This protective mechanism aligns with the cosmic censorship conjecture, positing that the unpredictable and often counterintuitive nature of singularities is masked within black holes, effectively safeguarding the integrity of physical predictions.

Conversely, the possibility of naked singularities—singularities not enclosed by an event horizon—could lead to profound implications for our understanding of cosmic order. Such singularities would allow for influence and visibility, wreaking havoc on established notions of causality and leading to potentially observable effects within the universe. An observer at a distance may witness the effects of these naked singularities, fundamentally altering traditional views on the behavior of gravity and spacetime. The existence of naked singularities introduces peculiar scenarios where, for example, light paths may be distorted or paths of particles could become chaotic, nullifying the predictability that general relativity asserts.

The investigation into the cosmic censorship conjecture and its ramifications extends beyond theoretical speculation; it stimulates critical discourse within the scientific community. While substantial support for the conjecture is provided through various mathematical proofs and models, questions abound regarding specific cases where cosmic censorship may break down. For instance, can singularities ever form without shielding themselves from view? Theoretical physicists continue to explore this domain by examining both classical and quantum perspectives, considering the implications of quantum gravity and string theory to present a more comprehensive picture of singularity formation and behavior.

One significant area of research contrasts the cosmic censorship conjecture with the principles of quantum mechanics. Quantum effects, such as entanglement and the behavior of virtual particles, could contribute to the circumstances in which naked singularities arise. Some physicists even posit that quantum gravitational effects might offer a new lens through which to evaluate the stability and properties of singularities. As such, research at the intersection of general relativity, quantum mechanics, and cosmology remains vital for understanding the ultimate fate of different gravitational systems and the consequences of singularity formation.

Moreover, the cosmic censorship conjecture stretches into philosophical realms, prompting inquiries into the nature of observation and reality itself. If naked singularities could exist alongside black holes, what does this mean for the fundamental fabric of spacetime and our understanding of the universe? The conjecture raises questions about determinism and allows for the exploration of unexplored realms of quantum phenomena that sit beyond our current grasp.

In conclusion, the cosmic censorship conjecture offers a compelling narrative that holds substantial implications for theoretical physics, cosmology, and philosophy. By proposing boundaries around singularities formed during gravitational collapse, this conjecture establishes a crucial framework for understanding the intricacies of spacetime and black hole dynamics. As researchers continue to probe the nuances of this conjecture, they advance the broader discourse surrounding the nature of existence and the universe, illuminating paths toward discovering the cosmic mysteries that lie beneath the surface of reality. The explorations into the cosmic censorship conjecture serve not only to deepen scientific inquiry but also to inspire reflections that stretch the limits of human understanding, reinforcing our relentless quest to unveil the secrets of the cosmos.

5. Real-World Proposals for Creating Wormholes

5.1. Theoretical Models of Construction

The exploration of the theoretical models of construction for wormholes encompasses a vibrant tapestry of scientific ingenuity and imaginative inquiry. As humanity stands on the threshold of cosmic exploration, the idea of constructing stable, traversable wormholes sparks excitement about the possibilities that lie beyond our current understanding of space and time. This subchapter delves into the hypothetical frameworks posited by physicists that detail how one might approach the conception of creating these extraordinary structures.

At the heart of the theoretical discussions surrounding wormhole construction is the understanding of general relativity, which forms the backbone of our knowledge regarding the shaping of spacetime by mass and energy. Wormholes, as hypothesized, consist of two mouths connected by a throat, acting as shortcuts through the fabric of the universe. However, the very nature of these connections brings about substantial challenges, particularly concerns surrounding stability and the requirements for exotic matter.

Exotic matter, characterized by negative energy density, is paramount in the dialogue about traversable wormholes. The concept emerges from the recognition that ordinary forms of matter cannot sustain the structural integrity of a wormhole; instead, it would collapse under the influence of its own gravity. Exotic matter acts as a counterbalance—an essential element that ensures the throat of the wormhole remains open to permit travel. Theoretical models posit that if sufficient quantities of exotic matter could be generated or discovered, it may be possible to stabilize a wormhole long enough for traversal.

One approach to generating exotic matter or fostering the conditions required for wormhole stability involves harnessing high-energy processes, such as those found in particle accelerators. Physicists posit that high-energy collisions between particles could give rise to transient states of negative energy density. Experiments designed to push the boundaries of particle physics may provide crucial insights into the formation and behavior of matter at very small scales—potentially leading to the discovery of specifics necessary for constructing wormholes.

The allure of cosmic strings—hypothetical one-dimensional topological defects in spacetime—also features prominently in theoretical models of wormhole construction. These objects, believed to have formed in the early universe, exhibit properties that could help stabilize wormholes if they exist. When two cosmic strings are brought close together, they warp the surrounding spacetime, creating conditions favorable for traversable wormholes. The interactions between cosmic strings offer rich terrain for theorists to explore, suggesting that the manipulation of such objects might lead to successful wormhole creation in a controlled environment.

Magnetic monopoles, hypothetical particles conceived in certain grand unified theories, also merit consideration in discussions of wormhole construction. Their unique characteristics, including the potential to exhibit properties of negative mass, render them enticing candidates for stabilizing wormholes. If such particles could be detected and harnessed, they might provide the critical framework to enable the creation of wormholes that allow for human exploration of distant reaches of the cosmos.

Both theoretical and experimental efforts to construct wormholes pose practical challenges that range from the need for extraordinary energy levels to the conception of technology that can accommodate the requisite conditions for manipulation of spacetime. The hurdles are considerable, including the challenge of generating and controlling exotic matter, as well as the engineering of devices capable of containing high-energy processes in a stable manner.

Other theoretical models propose experimental platforms to investigate the prospects of wormhole creation. These proposals aim to simulate the extreme conditions of spacetime manipulation through computer simulations or laboratory experiments that test the boundaries of current understanding. The development of advanced computational methods allows scientists to explore the interactions between various forms of matter and energy, granting insights that could ultimately inform real-world experimental designs.

Despite the uncertainties woven into the fabric of theoretical models, the pursuit of constructing wormholes inspires a profound sense of curiosity and creativity. As physicists develop and refine their models, the discussions surrounding the ethical implications of manipulating the cosmos come into sharp focus. The responsibility to explore the unknown must align with awareness of the potential consequences, embedding caution into the fervor for discovery.

In conclusion, the theoretical exploration of wormhole construction unveils a nexus of scientific inquiry that intertwines cutting-edge physics with the allure of speculative possibilities. From exotic matter to high-energy particle interactions, the models of construction engage with the complexities of the universe while pushing the boundaries of human understanding. As researchers continue to experiment, theorize, and expand their knowledge, the journey toward creating a stable wormhole is a poignant reminder of humanity's relentless aspiration to unlock the mysteries of the cosmos, inspiring future generations to dream of traversing the unharnessed pathways that lie in wait within the fabric of spacetime.

5.2. Lasers and High-Energy Particles

In the quest for understanding and possibly constructing wormholes, one of the pivotal areas of exploration is the role of lasers and high-energy particles. These advanced techniques aim to induce intense gravitational fields, thereby testing the theoretical frameworks behind wormhole formation and stability. The application of such technologies embodies a fusion of cutting-edge physics and innovative engineering, positioning them at the forefront of experimental approaches in wormhole research.

High-energy particles have the potential to significantly influence the spacetime fabric through their interactions. Particle accelerators, colossal machines that propel particles to near the speed of light, serve as vital tools in this exploration. By smashing particles together at high velocities, scientists create conditions mimicking those of the early universe, where extreme energies and densities may have allowed for phenomena such as wormhole-like structures to exist briefly. The collisions within these accelerators can generate new states of matter, including a focus on how exotic matter emerges, as it is theorized to play a critical role in the stability of traversable wormholes.

In tandem, lasers have emerged as another key player in the quest for wormhole research. Using high-intensity lasers can create localized gravitational fields through the techniques of laser plasma interactions. Lasers can focus enormous energy onto a very small area, potentially simulating conditions similar to those predicted around a wormhole. Researchers explore the idea of utilizing lasers to manipulate spacetime at a fundamental level. When directed into a vacuum, these high-powered beams generate phenomena like electromagnetic radiation and may even create localized spacetime disturbances that could be analogs to wormhole dynamics—offering insights into how matter and energy would behave under the influence of such cosmic constructs.

One notable proposal, still in the realm of theoretical exploration, suggests using high-energy lasers to create 'mini-wormholes' in laboratory settings. The concept involves generating short-lived wormhole-like structures by closely simulating the conditions necessary for traversability through the precise control of high-energy processes. If achieved, such experiments would not just provide empirical data regarding wormhole stability but would deepen our understanding of spacetime interactions governed by general relativity and quantum mechanics.

The interaction of high-energy particles and lasers can also serve as a testing ground for the implications surrounding exotic matter. The energy density produced during these high-energy collisions could, under extremely specific conditions, create states of negative energy densities—exotic matter that is essential for keeping wormholes stable. This potential discovery could transform existing theories on wormhole construction, leading physicists to explore whether it might indeed be feasible to either create or find exotic matter in observable events.

However, the utilization of lasers and high-energy particles for such ambitious objectives does not come without considerable challenges. Notably, the scientific community grapples with the engineering limitations in developing the precision instruments required to measure the desired effects at the required scales. The complexity surrounding the calculations and experimental designs must account for incredibly narrow tolerances, given the unstable nature of wormholes and the intricate behaviors of quantum fields.

Moreover, the ethical implications of high-energy particle experiments must also be navigated carefully. As researchers push the boundaries of physics, they must consider the potential consequences of manipulating fundamental forces that shape the cosmos. The unintended repercussions of advancing experiments in such uncharted territories call for a rigorous reflection on the responsibilities borne by scientific endeavors.

In conclusion, the exploration of lasers and high-energy particles as methods for inducing gravitational effects directly related to wormhole research presents an exciting vista within theoretical physics. The nuanced interactions between lasers and high-energy matter open avenues for future studies about warp in spacetime and transitions toward possible realities of traversable wormholes. Integrating these high-energy dynamics into research completes the broader understanding of wormholes—not as mere theoretical curiosities, but as possible phenomena that could reshape our knowledge of the universe. The path ahead is fraught with challenges, yet also filled with boundless potential as scientists sift through the layers of complexity that lay between theory and tangible discovery. This exploration not only fuels academic ambition but also evokes the universal curiosity at the heart of exploration—the desire to navigate and uncover the intricacies that exist within the cosmos.

5.3. Magnetic Monopoles

The exploration of magnetic monopoles—a theoretical particle that has yet to be discovered—offers intriguing possibilities for wormhole creation and stabilization. In conventional physics, magnetic poles always exist as dipoles, meaning that every magnet has both a north and a south pole. However, the concept of magnetic monopoles suggests the existence of isolated magnetic charges that would behave differently than the standard magnetic counterparts we are familiar with. The implications of magnetic monopoles are profound, particularly when considering their hypothetical role in the construction and stabilization of wormholes.

One of the most significant proposed benefits of magnetic monopoles in the context of wormhole theory lies in their potential to generate negative energy density. As previously discussed, exotic matter is crucial for maintaining the structural integrity of a traversable wormhole, counteracting collapse due to gravitational forces. If magnetic monopoles could indeed exhibit properties of negative energy density, they would offer a novel source of exotic matter—facilitating the stabilization of wormholes in a manner analogous to what exotic matter would accomplish.

The theoretical framework for magnetic monopoles emerges from various advanced physical theories, including Grand Unified Theories (GUTs) and string theory. These theories suggest mechanisms through which monopoles could arise from high-energy particle interactions, particularly during phase transitions in the early universe. If formed, these particles would interact with other particles in unique ways, including generating forced fields and influencing the topology of spacetime. These interactions could lead to localized effects, which may help support a traversable wormhole's structure by effectively modifying the gravitational environment around it.

Another aspect to consider is the relationship between magnetic monopoles and cosmic strings. Cosmic strings are hypothetical one-dimensional defects in spacetime predicted by certain theories of early universe cosmology. Some researchers propose that if magnetic monopoles exist, they could be intertwined with cosmic strings, amplifying their effects on spacetime and contributing to the construction of stable wormholes. The dual presence of monopoles and cosmic strings in the early universe may have facilitated the conditions necessary for wormhole formation, gifting researchers with a tantalizing avenue of exploration.

Furthermore, the potential detection of magnetic monopoles would ignite a flurry of research not only in theoretical physics but also in experimental investigations. If physicists could confirm the existence of magnetic monopoles and explore their properties, it would open up new frontiers in particle physics. Concurrently, research aimed at testing the fundamental principles of general relativity might yield insights into how magnetic monopoles could portray new forms of gravitational interactions, particularly in constructing traversable wormholes.

Despite the tantalizing prospects, it is essential to remain grounded when evaluating the ramifications of magnetic monopoles on wormhole stability. The singular nature of such particles is highly theoretical, with no experimental evidence currently affirming their existence. As such, while the overarching ideas are intellectually appealing, they remain speculative, pending rigorous scientific testing and validation.

In conclusion, the discussion surrounding magnetic monopoles presents a captivating layer in the multifaceted landscape of wormhole research. As theoretical constructs, they hold the promise of uncovering new realms of understanding about spacetime, exotic matter, and the fundamental forces that govern the universe. The interconnections between magnetic monopoles and wormhole stabilization reflect the ongoing quest of physics to expand our comprehension of the cosmos and challenge established paradigms. As research continues in this domain, magnetic monopoles may serve as a highlighting example of how theoretical physics can yield transformative ideas, beckoning us closer to the prospect of traversable wormholes and all the adventures they might entail.

5.4. Cosmic Strings

The concept of cosmic strings offers a tantalizing glimpse into potential methods for stabilizing and creating wormholes, further enriching the theoretical framework surrounding these enigmatic structures. Cosmic strings are hypothetical, one-dimensional defects that may have formed in the early universe due to symmetry-breaking phase transitions. Their existence is rooted in the principles of string theory and field theory, suggesting that when conditions in the universe were markedly different—milliseconds after the Big Bang— these strings could have emerged as solid loops extending across vast stretches of space.

The primary allure of cosmic strings lies in their predicted immense mass and the unique gravitational effects they could exert on surrounding spacetime. In essence, a cosmic string would create an intense gravitational field in its vicinity, warping the fabric of space-time around it. This characteristic could potentially be harnessed to stabilize a wormhole by utilizing the gravitational pull of these strings to counterbalance the collapse tendencies of wormhole throats. Theoretical models posit that if two cosmic strings were positioned closely together in spacetime, the warping effect could create a localized geometry conducive to the formation of a traversable wormhole.

If cosmic strings existed in the universe, they could serve as both anchors and catalysts for creating wormholes. Researchers theorize that arranging cosmic strings in specific configurations may generate distortions in spacetime robust enough to facilitate the necessary conditions for wormhole stabilization. For instance, placing two cosmic strings parallel to each other would theoretically create a region of spacetime where the gravitational influences could be balanced, providing a potential pathway for constructing wormholes that could be traversed.

Moreover, the nature of cosmic strings as energy sources might also shed light on the possibilities of exotic matter. The properties of cosmic strings could interact with other forms of matter and energy, and if they were capable of producing regions of negative energy density (as theorized), they would significantly bolster the feasibility of constructing traversable wormholes. The interplay between these strings and exotic matter would be essential in forming a stable throat, allowing safe passage for whatever—or whoever—ventured through.

The theoretical underpinning of cosmic strings is further enhanced by their implications in high-energy scenarios, such as those created in particle accelerators or astrophysical events. Scientists could look for evidence of cosmic strings through cosmic microwave background radiation or gravitational wave detections, as their influence might create observable phenomena indicative of their existence. Discovering cosmic strings would not only serve to enhance our understanding of cosmology but also offer practical avenues toward realizing the constructs necessary for wormholes.

However, despite the tantalizing possibilities cosmic strings offer, they remain purely theoretical at present. There are several outstanding questions within the scientific community regarding their actual existence and the conditions required to study these defects in a laboratory or astrophysical setting. The pursuit of answers surrounding cosmic strings involves advanced theoretical modeling, experimental designs, and observational strategies—each domain requiring significant interdisciplinary collaboration across physics.

Consequently, while cosmic strings provide an intriguing pathway for considering the construction and stabilization of wormholes, they encapsulate the broader challenges present in modern physics. As scientists endeavor to unravel the mysteries of the universe and come to grips with the vast cosmic order, the concept of cosmic strings serves as a lighthouse guiding inquiry into the phenomena that could once be reserved for the realm of science fiction but may one day hold real scientific merit.

The exploration of cosmic strings not only enhances the scientific narratives surrounding wormhole research but also invites philosophical inquiries about the very nature of the universe. If these extraordinary defects exist and if they hold the key to bridging cosmic distances, what does that say about our understanding of reality? The investigations into cosmic strings and their implications for wormholes continue to inspire the imaginations of scientists and dreamers alike. As the threads connecting these ideas continue to intertwine, they beckon humanity to look deeper into the cosmos and question the vast potential lying just beyond our understanding.

5.5. Practical Challenges

The prospect of creating and utilizing wormholes as travel conduits through spacetime is an enthralling and complex venture, riddled with practical challenges that span both scientific and engineering domains. The theoretical constructs suggest tantalizing possibilities for interstellar travel and even time travel; however, implementing these ideas into a workable reality raises numerous hurdles that scientists and engineers must navigate.

At the forefront of these challenges lies the need to stabilize a wormhole. The foundational idea of a wormhole hinges on the notion of two mouths connected by a throat. While this concept may exist elegantly in theoretical frameworks, the reality is that traversable wormholes would be subject to immense gravitational forces that threaten to collapse them almost instantaneously upon formation. Current theories indicate that ordinary matter alone cannot sufficiently counteract these forces—instead, the presence of exotic matter, which possesses negative energy density, is deemed essential for maintaining the stability of a traversable wormhole.

Exotic matter remains a key hurdle within this endeavor; it has not been empirically demonstrated to exist in the quantities required for practical applications. Theoretical physics suggests possibilities for exotic matter to arise through quantum fluctuations or other means, but definitive evidence and methods for its generation are largely speculative. Thus, the search for exotic matter remains a pressing challenge, one that necessitates novel approaches to particle physics and energy manipulation.

Turning attention to the engineering side, the machinery and technology needed to create, maintain, and traverse a wormhole are currently beyond our capabilities. The energies and materials required to construct such structures would demand advancements in our understanding of physics and engineering principles. For instance, the development of particle accelerators capable of achieving the energies necessary to create conditions for wormhole stabilization would require unprecedented advancements in technology. These machines would have to be designed to produce and contain exotic matter while simultaneously achieving the required high energy and precision to manipulate spacetime.

The potential locations for the construction of wormholes also pose geographical and logistical challenges. A wormhole's stability might depend on its environment and proximity to other bodies with substantial mass. The potential electromagnetic and gravitational influences from nearby celestial phenomena must be factored into any proposal for its construction. Understanding the implications of such environmental factors is critical in developing predictive models for wormhole stability and traversal.

Moreover, theoretical discussions about the collapse mechanisms of wormholes give rise to sophisticated problems involving quantum mechanics and general relativity. There is an ongoing discourse concerning how quantum effects may come into play in determining the ultimate fate of a wormhole. The potential for wormholes to be affected by Hawking radiation—as seen with black holes—demands rigorous examination. Whether wormholes would succumb to similar mechanisms of energy loss, leading to collapse, is an aspect requiring profound exploration.

Additionally, considerations surrounding the traveler's safety raise important technical questions. Scientists must contemplate the conditions one might face when entering a wormhole. For instance, what kinds of radiation exposure, gravitational forces, or other unpredictable physical phenomena would impact human travelers? The implications surrounding this area bring black holes and their effects into the discussion; research into the extreme environmental conditions present in those contexts may inform our understanding of wormhole traversal.

Lastly, ethical considerations arise both in the methodologies proposed to explore the creation of wormholes and in pondering humanity's first steps into such unknown territories. Deliberations about the consequences of traversing wormholes—whether physical, social, or philosophical—necessitate a balanced approach, weighing scientific curiosity against potential risks to human safety and the broader implications of altering our place in the universe.

In summary, the challenges associated with creating and traversing wormholes are profound and multifaceted. The combination of theoretical constraints, the search for exotic matter, engineering limitations, environmental interactions, and ethical implications constructs a landscape filled with both intrigue and complexity. As research advances and technology evolves, ongoing efforts to address these challenges will determine whether the dream of wormhole travel becomes a tangible reality or remains an imaginative concept primarily explored in science fiction narratives. The journey toward understanding and potentially harnessing the power of wormholes represents one of the most exhilarating challenges within modern physics—an endeavor that could reshape our understanding of the cosmos and our place within it.

6. Fictional Depictions of Wormholes

6.1. Wormholes in Literature

The portrayal of wormholes in literature is a rich and varied tapestry, reflecting humanity's fascination with the unknown, the cosmic, and the potential for extraordinary journeys through time and space. From foundational works of science fiction that framed the conceptual boundaries of wormholes to contemporary narratives that explore their implications, literature offers a multidimensional lens through which to examine these theoretical constructs.

One of the earliest mentions of wormhole-like structures can be traced back to the works of science fiction pioneer H.G. Wells. In his seminal work, "The Time Machine," published in 1895, Wells introduced readers to the concept of time travel, although he did not specifically mention wormholes. His exploration of time as a dimension that could be navigated much like space laid the groundwork for future authors to delve into the ideas of non-linear time and alternate realities.

The notion of wormholes as actual constructs was popularized in science fiction literature by authors like Carl Sagan and his celebrated work, "Contact," published in 1985. In this novel, Sagan illustrated a scenario in which humanity makes contact with extraterrestrial intelligence via a mysterious wormhole. The detailed scientific framework and potential for real-world implications provided a strong basis for subsequent explorations of the concept in both science and fiction. Sagan's work emphasized the idea that wormholes could serve as bridges across the vast distances of space, challenging the perceived boundaries of human exploration.

Another pivotal contribution came from physicist Kip Thorne's "The Science of Interstellar," which accompanied Christopher Nolan's film "Interstellar." Thorne's work meticulously blended scientific theory and narrative, making wormholes accessible to a broader audience. His explanations not only depicted wormholes as potential avenues for time travel but also explored the implications of traveling through such structures, offering readers a glimpse into the intersection of reality and imagination.

Literary works such as Greg Egan's "Permutation City" and "Quarantine" delve into the philosophical and existential implications of wormholes and virtual realities. Egan's narrative imagination stretches the boundaries of what it means to exist and challenges conceptions of identity through the lens of advanced technology and the potential manipulation of spacetime. Such explorations invite readers to consider the implications of human consciousness and technology while intertwining scientific concepts with profound existential inquiries.

Contemporary authors have further embraced wormholes as narrative devices to tackle themes of exploration, identity, and the unforeseen consequences of human curiosity. For instance, in "The Long Way to a Small, Angry Planet" by Becky Chambers, wormholes serve not just as pathways through space but as elements of community and connection among diverse species. Chambers' depiction highlights the relational aspects of exploration, inviting readers to reflect on the interpersonal dimensions of embarking on cosmic journeys.

Wormholes have also become prominent in young adult literature, such as in "A Wrinkle in Time" by Madeleine L'Engle, where the concept of tesseracts—hypothetical structures that allow characters to move through space and time—is introduced. Though not explicitly labeled as wormholes, they capture the essence of traversing dimensions and demonstrate how young readers grapple with concepts of science and adventure within imaginative frameworks.

Overall, wormholes in literature transcend mere theoretical constructs, evolving into powerful symbols that reflect society's hopes, fears, and aspirations related to exploration and understanding of the universe. The narratives portrayed not only embody technological possibilities but also challenge readers to ponder the ethical implications and consequences of wielding such power. Through the lens of literary imagination, wormholes become portals—not only to distant worlds but also to deeper examinations of what it means to be human in an expansive cosmos.

In essence, the narratives surrounding wormholes have grown to encompass not just the mechanics of theoretical physics but also vibrant explorations of the human condition, intertwining scientific conjecture with philosophical inquiry. As literature continues to evolve in response to advancements in our understanding of the cosmos, the exploration of wormholes promises to remain a rich vein of creativity and thought for generations of readers to come.

6.2. Cinema's Adaptation

The depiction of wormholes in cinema showcases a fascinating intersection of science and imagination, reflecting the cultural significance of these enigmatic structures. Filmmakers often take creative liberties with the concept, using wormholes as vessels through which characters embark on grand adventures, traverse time, or explore the unknown.

One of the most iconic representations of wormholes is found in Christopher Nolan's "Interstellar." The film beautifully marries theoretical physics with emotional storytelling, as characters use a traversable wormhole located near Saturn to access another galaxy. The portrayal of the wormhole itself—a swirling tunnel of light—captures the awe of interstellar travel while grounding its narrative in scientific principles, largely thanks to the involvement of physicist Kip Thorne as a consultant. Thorne's contributions ensure that the visual effects portraying the wormhole adhere as closely as possible to the theories of general relativity, offering audiences a glimpse of what such a cosmic construct could look like.

Similarly, the animated series "Rick and Morty" employs wormholes as a plot device to facilitate the show's wild adventures across dimensions and timelines. The series leverages humor and absurdity while exploring complex themes of existence and consequence, allowing viewers to reflect on the implications of traversing wormholes—even in a comedic setting. The show's approach highlights how wormholes can serve as metaphors for unpredictability and chaos, resonating with viewers who enjoy narratives that blend thought-provoking concepts with entertainment.

In "The Abyss," directed by James Cameron, the notion of a wormhole is introduced through the exploration of deep-sea environments as characters encounter an alien species capable of manipulating water to create portals. Here, wormholes emphasize humanity's relationship with the unknown and our capacity for exploration, drawing parallels to our desire to understand both the cosmos and the depths of our oceans. The film's treatment of wormholes as conduits for communication and understanding echoes a broader cultural yearning for connection across vast distances.

Wormholes also emerge as central themes in films like "Contact," where a scientist, played by Jodie Foster, utilized a theoretical construct akin to a wormhole to reach out to extraterrestrial intelligences. The film emphasizes the quest for knowledge and human connection, utilizing the concept of wormholes to explore themes of destiny and purpose. It prompts viewers to ponder the significance of exploration in our understanding of the cosmos, as well as the potential for contact with other forms of existence.

Another notable example is the American science fiction television series "Stargate," which showcases a different approach to the concept of wormholes through its portrayals of the Stargate, a device that connects two distant locations, effectively forming a stable wormhole. The imaginative storytelling of "Stargate" embraces the possibilities of interstellar travel while encouraging philosophical reflections on our place within a larger universe.

Beyond storytelling, the visual effects associated with wormholes in film play a significant role in shaping public perception of these complex scientific ideas. The swirling designs, vibrant colors, and dynamic movement within wormholes create a visceral experience that sparks interest and imagination. Such artistic interpretations contribute to a collective cultural fascination with the mysteries of the universe, encouraging viewers to engage with the underlying scientific concepts.

The narrative power of cinema ensures that wormholes emerge as metaphorical tools reflecting humanity's innate desire for exploration and understanding. With each film, creators invite audiences to contemplate the implications of traversing these pathways through spacetime—not just as vehicles for adventure but as symbols of curiosity, innovation, and the profound mysteries that lie beyond the stars.

As the realm of cinematic depictions of wormholes continues to evolve, it fuels a dialogue that transcends science fiction. These portrayals challenge viewers to explore the boundaries of possibility, creating a dynamic interplay between factual science and imaginative narratives that inspires future generations of scientists, thinkers, and storytellers alike. Thus, as filmmakers push the boundaries of storytelling through the lens of wormholes, they deepen our understanding of the cosmos and enrich our collective imagination, ensuring that the legacy of these cosmic bridges persists in cultural memory.

6.3. Television and Serial Narratives

In the realm of television, the treatment of wormholes has served as both a fascinating narrative device and a platform for exploring complex themes of time, space, and existence. Numerous popular series have woven the concept of wormholes into their story arcs, allowing for imaginative explorations that engage viewers in speculative philosophies and thrilling adventures. This subchapter will delve into some of the most notable representations of wormholes in television, examining how these narratives resonate with broader scientific concepts and cultural curiosities.

A cornerstone in the portrayal of wormholes can be found in the sci-fi series "Stargate SG-1." The show introduces the Stargate, a sophisticated device capable of creating stable wormholes between two distant points in space. The Stargate serves not only as the central plot device for interstellar travel but also encourages exploration of alien cultures, existential threats, and the moral implications of advanced technology. The way the series integrates wormholes into its narrative framework highlights the possibilities of connectivity and the adventure inherent in exploring unknown worlds. Audiences are captivated by the prospect of traversing vast distances in the blink of an eye, fueled by a spirit of discovery and adventure.

"Doctor Who," a seminal science fiction series, also features the use of wormholes—albeit in a more fluid and nuanced manner. The Doctor's TARDIS, a time-traveling spacecraft, utilizes a form of "time vortex" that enables traversal through both time and space. While not strictly described as a traditional wormhole, the TARDIS embodies the spirit of interconnectivity that wormholes symbolize—offering characters possibilities limited only by their imagination. Through various adventures, the series explores the implications of time travel, the responsibilities that come with such power, and the ethical dilemmas encountered when meddling with time and history. The infinite time-lines and the effect of individual choices echo philosophical inquiries about fate and free will, deeply resonating with viewers.

"Younger," a modern take on intergenerational challenges, features episodes that subtly incorporate scientific principles inspired by wormhole theories, emphasizing the intertwining of time, memory, and identity. The characters experience lessons that mirror the un-predictability of traveling through a wormhole, navigating personal relationships through sensitive conflicts and reconciliations. The show invites viewers to reflect on the concept of time as it relates to personal growth and identity, mirroring the adventures through wormholes within the cosmic framework.

In the animated series "Rick and Morty," wormholes are often utilized as comedic devices to thrust characters into wild, unpredictable situations across time and space. The show cleverly employs these constructs to explore the absurdity of existence while also provid-ing commentary on scientific concepts. By prioritizing humor over realism, the series engages audiences with a playful yet thought-provoking representation of interdimensional travel. The show's narrative invites viewers to consider philosophical dilemmas, such as the implications of multiple realities and the insignificance of individual actions in an unfathomable multiverse.

Another significant entry is "The Expanse," which addresses wormholes within a hard science fiction framework. The series introduces the concept of "the Ring," a massive structure that serves as a gateway for travel between solar systems, effectively acting as a wormhole of sorts. The show emphasizes the geopolitical ramifications of interstellar travel and the potential ethical quandaries that could arise around the resources tied to wormhole access. This sober representation encourages viewers to grapple with issues of conflict, colonization, and the complexities that accompany advanced technologies.

The portrayal of wormholes in television can influence societal perceptions of science and philosophy, sparking curiosity about astrophysical concepts while simultaneously providing vehicles for introspection. By integrating wormholes into their narratives, creators can illustrate the vast possibilities of exploration beyond the confines of known reality, beckoning viewers into a speculative future enriched by the quest for understanding and discovery. These narratives invite audiences to engage with fundamental questions about existence, identity, and the implications of traversing the unknown, ultimately connecting the scientific imagination with the essence of what it means to be human.

In summary, wormholes function as potent narrative devices across a variety of television series, serving to challenge perceptions of time, space, and reality itself. Through their imaginative representations, these shows provoke discussions about the philosophical implications of their cosmic constructs while simultaneously thrilling viewers with tales of adventure and exploration. As technology advances and scientific understanding deepens, the cultural impact of such narratives promises to resonate in the collective consciousness, inspiring new generations to ponder the possibilities of the universe.

6.4. Visual Arts and Wormholes

The visual representation of wormholes in the arts serves as a powerful conduit for human imagination and cultural exploration, transcending the boundaries of scientific theory to become a potent symbol of possibility, adventure, and the unknown. The portrayal of wormholes in both traditional visual arts and contemporary digital media captures the fascination that these theoretical constructs incite, inviting audiences to engage with complex ideas through aesthetic expressions.

In the realm of traditional visual arts, wormholes have often been depicted through abstract paintings, sculptures, and installations that evoke the experience of traversing through cosmic dimensions. Artists utilize swirling forms, vibrant colors, and dynamic compositions to convey the sense of movement and the distortion of spacetime associated with wormhole travel. For example, the use of spirals and vortices can symbolize the rapid transport from one location to another, while contrasting shades may represent the duality of existence across different realms or timelines. These artistic interpretations not only serve to visualize scientific concepts but also allow for personal and emotional interpretations that resonate with viewers on a deeper level.

The emergence of digital art has further revolutionized how wormholes are represented, allowing for immersive experiences that draw audiences into the heart of cosmic phenomena. Virtual reality (VR) and augmented reality (AR) applications create participatory environments where viewers can navigate through simulated wormholes, offering firsthand experiences of transcending space and time. Through these interactive platforms, audiences become active participants in the narrative, able to explore the intricacies of these dimensional gateways in profoundly personal ways. This engagement with digital art extends the dialogue between science and creativity, provoking questions about our understanding of the universe and our place within it.

Cinema has long been a primary vessel for visualizing wormholes, popularizing speculative concepts through compelling narratives and cutting-edge visual effects. The stunning representations of wormholes in films like "Interstellar," with its spiraling, luminescent visuals, capture the awe of cosmic exploration and reinforce the theoretical underpinnings presented by physicists like Kip Thorne. The blending of scientific accuracy with imaginative storytelling not only captivates audience attention but also sparks curiosity about the realities of wormhole physics, inviting viewers to consider the profound implications of traversing such pathways.

Television series also delve into the visualizations of wormholes, using serialized narratives to explore their possibilities within varied contexts. Shows like "Doctor Who" and "Stargate SG-1" employ visually dynamic representations of wormholes, creating memorable images associated with travel across time and space. These depictions evoke intrigue and wonder, encouraging discussions about the theoretical nature of wormholes while simultaneously engaging the audience's sense of adventure and exploration.

Moreover, the influence of modern technologies—such as computer graphics and simulations—expands the potential for portrayals of wormholes. Scientific visualization tools can simulate the effects of gravitational fields and spacetime distortions, generating visual aids that help researchers and educators illustrate complex concepts. These tools pave the way for a more profound public engagement with the science of wormholes, transforming abstract theoretical constructs into comprehensible, tangible, and visually captivating elements that inspire wonder.

The cultural impact of visual art representations of wormholes extends beyond the realm of science fiction and creative imagination; they touch on broader existential themes that resonate with the human experience. Images of wormholes can symbolize humanity's quest for knowledge and understanding, encapsulating the innate drive to explore not only the outer cosmos but also the depths of the self. As viewers navigate through depictions of cosmic pathways, they are invited to reflect on their own journeys, aspirations, and existential questions about time, reality, and the possibility of limitless exploration.

In conclusion, the artistic representation of wormholes plays a multifaceted role that bridges the realms of science, philosophy, and culture. From traditional visual arts to contemporary digital media, these portrayals engage audiences in imaginative explorations of theoretical constructs, provoking deeper reflections on our understanding of the universe and our place within it. As society continues to grapple with the mysteries of spacetime and the implications of advanced physics, the artistic interpretations of wormholes will remain a vital part of the cultural dialogue, inspiring generations to dream of possibilities that extend far beyond the known horizons of reality.

6.5. The Role of Imagination

Imagination plays a crucial role in shaping our understanding of complex scientific concepts such as wormholes, transforming abstract theories into vivid narratives that resonate with both the scientific community and the broader public. The interplay of scientific inquiry and imaginative speculation serves as a catalyst for exploration, propelling ideas related to wormhole travel from the realm of theoretical physics into captivating stories, enticing readers and viewers alike.

The allure of wormholes lies in their promise of traversing vast expanses of space and time, capturing the human imagination with the possibility of instantaneous travel to distant galaxies or even alternate realities. This fascination is reflected in the burgeoning genre of science fiction, where writers and filmmakers can manipulate these constructs for thrilling adventures or profound ethical dilemmas. Through their narratives, creators harness wormholes as symbols of exploration and the unknown—a representation of humanity's enduring quest to understand the universe and our place within it.

In literature, for instance, authors have envisioned wormholes as gateways to infinite possibilities, allowing characters to traverse through time and space, challenge the nature of fate, and confront the consequences of their choices. Such narratives engage readers with the implications of time travel and the interconnectedness of lives across parallel dimensions, forcing them to grapple with philosophical inquiries about identity and existence. Iconic works encourage audiences to reconsider their perceptions of reality—making them think beyond linear time and exploring the potential interpretations of their personal journeys against a cosmic backdrop.

Film and television have further expanded the societal perception of wormholes. By providing compelling visual representations of these constructs, filmmakers evoke awe and intrigue in viewers. Movies like "Interstellar," with its scientifically grounded portrayal of a traversable wormhole, not only educate audiences about complex principles of physics but also humanize the concepts through relatable characters and emotional narratives. These visual adaptations cultivate public interest in scientific topics, inspiring a new generation of dreamers and scientists eager to explore the intricacies of the cosmos.

The role of imagination doesn't stop at entertainment. It also informs the scientific process itself by inspiring researchers to explore uncharted territories, question established frameworks, and innovate beyond current knowledge. Many theoretical physicists advocate for bold thinking in a discipline often constrained by empirical data and conventional wisdom. Theoretical models, including some associated with wormholes, originate from speculative thoughts about the nature of spacetime, pushing the boundaries of established science and inviting further investigation into the unknown.

Moreover, as scientific advancements reveal insights about the universe, there is a reciprocal relationship between science and imagination, as emerging discoveries often beckon new narratives in popular culture. The continuous evolution of theories related to wormholes invites creators to devise even more intricate stories, allowing the interplay of scientific thought and imaginative exploration to flourish. This synergy fosters a broader public fascination with astrophysics, encouraging interdisciplinary collaborations that span literature, cinema, philosophy, and scientific discovery—deepening our collective understanding of the cosmos.

In conclusion, imagination is a driving force behind the narratives we construct around wormhole travel, shaping public interest and scientific discourse alike. As we engage with speculative ideas and envision what lies beyond the confines of our current understanding, we not only entertain ourselves but also challenge preconceived notions of reality, identity, and existence. The stories we tell about wormholes reflect a profound and ancient desire to explore the unknown, propelling humanity further into the vast expanse of the universe as we forge a path toward realizing the potential that lies within our imagination.

7. The Cultural Impact of Wormhole Travel

7.1. Societal Fascination with Wormholes

In the modern era, the concept of wormholes has become a subject of immense fascination and speculation, epitomizing humanity's intrinsic desire to explore the cosmos and challenge the limitations of our existence. This societal fascination with wormholes transcends scientific circles, permeating popular culture, literature, cinema, and even philosophical inquiry. As theorists and dreamers ponder the possibility of traversing these cosmic bridges, the implications paint a rich tapestry of potential realities that inspire diverse reflections on the nature of time, space, and human ambition.

The allure of wormholes can be traced back to the foundational ideas introduced by physicists in the early 20th century. When Albert Einstein proposed the framework of general relativity, it laid the groundwork for exploring concepts that transcended the classical understanding of space and time. This revolutionary perspective opened the door to imagining shortcuts through the fabric of the universe, encapsulated in the theoretical constructs of the Einstein-Rosen Bridge and, later, the more robust models proposed by contemporary physicists. The very idea that one could traverse vast distances or journey across time in an instant ignited excitement among scientists and the general public alike.

Wormholes have since become embedded in the collective imagination, serving as compelling symbols of exploration, adventure, and the unknown. Provocative narratives and stunning visual representations in popular culture have contributed to the widespread fascination, elevating wormhole theory from an esoteric scientific discussion to a widely recognized motif within literature and film. Works like "Interstellar" and series such as "Stargate" introduce these constructs to audiences, demonstrating their potential for travel and the profound implications of manipulating the spacetime continuum. Such portrayals, while speculative, encapsulate humanity's enduring curiosity about the cosmos and our place within it.

The societal fascination with wormholes also reflects deep philosophical inquiries surrounding existence, reality, and determinism. If wormholes were to exist, the potential for time travel raises compelling questions about causality, free will, and the nature of reality itself. Can past events be altered, or is history immutable? How would the ability to traverse time and space affect human experience, identity, and agency? These inquiries delve into the realms of ethics and morality as considerations about the consequences of manipulating time intertwine with the adventure of exploration.

Furthermore, as scientists continue to work toward understanding the theoretical underpinnings of wormholes, the public's interest remains steadfast. The advancements in physics and the ongoing discourse about exotic matter, stability, and traversability fuel a cumulative curiosity that propels both technological and cultural exploration. Investments in scientific research and expanded funding for theoretical studies signal a recognition of the broader impact open inquiries into wormholes may have—not only on cosmology but on human understanding and connection to the universe.

The conversation surrounding wormholes also serves as a bridge between science fiction and science fact. Just as the theoretical concepts originating from academia inspire imaginative narratives, the stories crafted in fiction, in turn, influence the scientific community's pursuit. As narratives explore the implications of wormholes, they invite scientists to keep pushing boundaries, expanding their inquiries into the unknown and acknowledging the possibilities that lie beyond current understanding.

In exploring the societal fascination with wormholes, one recognizes the interplay between scientific pursuit and human imagination, showcasing the richness of both disciplines. The narratives encapsulate our hopes, dreams, and fears, reflecting our desire for transcendence and understanding of the cosmos. As more people engage with the idea of wormhole travel, whether through literature, film, or philosophical discourse, it reaffirms the significance of the human quest for knowledge and our determination to explore the mysteries that await us. Thus, society's fascination with wormholes represents not just a scientific curiosity, but a profound reflection of what it means to be human in a universe filled with possibilities.

7.2. Wormholes and Popular Science

The exploration of wormholes in the context of popular science has played a vital role in demystifying complex scientific concepts for the public while simultaneously stirring excitement and curiosity about the possibilities of time and space travel. As theoretical physics continues to advance, the portrayal of wormholes through accessible narratives enables laypeople to grasp the fundamental ideas underpinning these cosmic constructs, fostering a broader appreciation of fundamental physics and its implications for our understanding of the universe.

One significant contribution of popular science to the discourse surrounding wormholes is the effort to translate complex scientific ideas into relatable language and imagery. Authors, educators, and science communicators have undertaken the challenge of making the abstract concepts of general relativity and quantum mechanics approachable. Through engaging metaphors, vivid illustrations, and stimulating narratives, these communicators have effectively captured the imagination of audiences, transforming theoretical discussions into stories that resonate on a human level. By providing analogies that relate to everyday experiences, popular science facilitates a deeper understanding of how wormholes might function as shortcuts through spacetime and the potential for connecting distant points in the cosmos.

Television shows, documentaries, and films have become indispensable tools in popularizing wormhole theories, showcasing them as captivating scientific possibilities. Presentations on platforms such as PBS's "NOVA" or popular science channels have explored the foundational principles of wormholes, inviting experts to share their insights in an accessible manner. Such programs not only illuminate the scientific theories regarding wormholes but also ponder the radical implications for time travel and our understanding of the universe.

By presenting concepts through visually compelling formats, these narratives serve to ignite wonder and inquiry, prompting audiences to engage with subjects that might otherwise seem daunting.

Literature has also provided a significant avenue for popular science to flourish in relation to wormholes. Writers like Carl Sagan, Kip Thorne, and Greg Egan have adeptly intertwined scientific principles with narrative storytelling in their works, offering readers a captivating blend of fact and fiction. By embedding scientific concepts within compelling narratives, these authors inspire dialogue about the future of space exploration and the ethical considerations that accompany it. Moreover, the marriage between fiction and science serves to stimulate interest in actual scientific inquiry, driving public passion for understanding the nature of the universe and the intricacies of wormholes.

Moreover, societal fascination with wormholes reveals a deeper yearning for exploration and the unknown. People are drawn to the potential for transcending the confines of our physical limitations and imagining a reality in which travel across vast distances or even time becomes possible. This notion evokes wonder, igniting curiosity not only about the mechanics of wormholes but also about the philosophical implications of such explorations—inviting considerations of identity, existence, and our place in the cosmos. The dialogue surrounding wormholes encourages a wider interest in foundational physics, ultimately fostering appreciation for the broader scientific endeavor.

However, popular science also serves to usher in skepticism and critical examination concerning the implications of wormhole travel. As discussions unfold about traversing dimensions and manipulating time, questions about causality, paradoxes, and the moral implications of such extraordinary power arise. Popular media often foregrounds these debates, ensuring that audiences engage with the complexities of these concepts while reflecting on the potential consequences of real-world advancements in theoretical physics. By addressing these challenges transparently, popular science cultivates a nuanced understanding of wormholes that goes beyond mere fascination, prompting reflections on their role in shaping human destiny and identity.

In summary, popular science has a multifaceted role in promoting and demystifying the concept of wormholes, translating complex theories into narratives that resonate with the public and inspire curiosity. By leveraging accessible storytelling, visual media, and engaging discourse, popular science fosters an appreciation for the wonders of the universe while simultaneously encouraging critical reflection on the implications of exploring the unknown. As humanity continues to probe the depths of theoretical inquiry, the interplay between popular science and wormhole exploration remains an essential force in shaping our understanding of the cosmos and our aspirations for future discoveries.

7.3. Philosophical Implications

The exploration of wormholes transcends mere theoretical constructs, inviting profound contemplation within the realms of philosophy and ethics. As our understanding of these exotic entities—potential cosmic shortcuts through space and time—grows, so too does the responsibility to ponder their implications on our understanding of existence, identity, and morality. The philosophical discourse surrounding wormholes is animated by several foundational questions, revealing the intricate interplay between scientific inquiry and the ethical dimensions of exploration.

At the heart of philosophical discussions about wormhole travel lies the fascinating challenge posed to our understanding of time and causality. If a traversable wormhole exists, it might allow for journeys that transcend the linear progression of time, leading to scenarios with significant ramifications. The possibility of traveling backwards in time raises profound inquiries about the nature of reality. Would events become mutable, allowing for alterations of the past? If so, what would this mean for our understanding of fate and free will? The implications of time travel through wormholes encourage us to consider how our actions shape existence, posing essential questions about the interconnections between agency, morality, and destiny.

Furthermore, the concept of parallel universes presents another philosophical layer to the discussion surrounding wormholes. If these cosmic structures serve as gateways to alternate realities or timelines, it raises profound inquiries about alternative histories and the existence of parallel lives. What does it mean to traverse through a conduit into a universe where different choices were made or events unfolded? This consideration invites reflections on identity and the multiplicity of selves, probing our understanding of who we are if alternate versions of our lives exist in diverse realities.

The ethical implications inherent in wormhole travel provoke critical examination of our responsibilities as we contemplate such profound technologies. If humanity were capable of traveling through wormholes, the potential to alter historical events poses ethical dilemmas of monumental consequences. Questions of consent, responsibility, and accountability arise. Would it be justifiable to intervene in past actions that bear significant ethical ramifications? The potential to manipulate timelines beckons us to weigh the morality of wielding such extraordinary power against the value of preserving historical integrity.

The exploration of wormholes also raises concerns regarding human responsibility toward environmental and cosmic stewardship. As we embark on journeys through the cosmos, we must contemplate the consequences of our actions on celestial bodies, ecosystems, and potentially intelligent life. The ethical discourse surrounding discovery must encompass considerations of how exploration may impact the universes we traverse, urging a conscientious approach to the unknown, similar to discussions surrounding environmental ethics in our contemporary world.

Moreover, the philosophical discourse surrounding wormhole travel intertwines with themes of existential inquiry and the nature of existence itself. The potential to traverse realities compellingly probes the boundaries of human experience and our understanding of the temporal flow of life. Just as we encounter the mysteries of existence on a personal level, the act of traveling through wormholes invites us to consider our place in a grander cosmic narrative, igniting reflections on the interconnectedness of lives across time and space.

In conclusion, the philosophical implications surrounding wormhole travel are vast and multifaceted, engaging with fundamental questions about time, reality, morality, and existence. As we navigate the terrain of scientific exploration, it is essential to remain cognizant of the responsibilities that accompany such advancements. The dialogue surrounding the potential for wormhole travel serves to open pathways not merely in the cosmos but within our understanding of the ethical landscape that shapes our decisions in the present and will continue to influence our trajectory into the infinite possibilities of the future. At the crossroads of science, philosophy, and ethics, the inquiry into wormholes invites all of us to engage thoughtfully with the mysteries that lie ahead.

7.4. Ethical Considerations

Wormhole travel, a captivating concept that intertwines the realms of science, philosophy, and ethics, presents a series of intricate ethical considerations that provoke rigorous debate among scientists, ethicists, and the general public. As the theoretical possibility of traversing these cosmic bridges tantalizes our collective imagination, it simultaneously raises profound questions about the implications of such a transformative ability and the responsibilities that accompany it.

At the forefront of the ethical discourse is the potential for time travel through wormholes. The prospect of traveling backward in time beckons inquiries into causality and the nature of reality. Should humans possess the ability to alter past events, the consequences could be staggering. Philosophically, this challenge crystallizes into infamous paradoxes, such as the grandfather paradox, wherein a time traveler could inadvertently prevent their own existence. The ethical dilemma emerges: if the ability to intervene in the past existed, would it be morally justifiable to do so? The potential ramifications of changing historical events necessitate careful consideration, as such actions could alter the course of history in unforeseeable and potentially detrimental ways.

The exploration of alternate realities and parallel universes further complicates ethical considerations related to wormhole travel. If traversable wormholes indeed exist, their potential to lead to alternate timelines introduces the possibility of multiple forms of existence. The decision to engage with a new reality would raise consequential questions about identity, continuity, and moral responsibility. What does it mean for an individual to traverse different realities where alternative choices are made? The existence of parallel lives challenges our notions of selfhood and morality, prompting reflections on how one navigates their ethical obligations across multiple timelines.

Additionally, the implications of environmental stewardship become pronounced when considering the capabilities afforded by wormhole travel. As humanity reaches toward cosmic exploration, the potential impact on extraterrestrial ecosystems or civilizations must be weighed against the quest for knowledge and discovery. Ethical considerations surrounding our responsibilities to protect other worlds become increasingly relevant as the boundaries of exploration expand. Questions about consent, the ethics of interaction, and the impact on inevitably vulnerable extraterrestrial environments merit thoughtful discourse, as humanity wrestles with the potential consequences of wielding such power.

As we contemplate the societal implications of wormhole travel, the equal access and equitable distribution of such technology emerge as critical ethical challenges. The potential for wormholes to revolutionize travel and exploration could also reinforce existing societal inequalities if access remains limited to particular groups or nations. Moral considerations surrounding the democratization of advanced technology prompt discussions on how to ensure responsible governance and equitable access, avoiding the pitfalls of exploitation or monopolization that might emerge within the pursuit of such capabilities.

The emergence of ethical questions surrounding artificial intelligence (AI) also cannot be ignored. If AI systems are tasked with managing or facilitating wormhole travel, questions arise about the ethical framework guiding their decision-making processes. What responsibilities do developers and operators have in ensuring safe and equitable use? The integration of AI in the exploratory process precipitates critical discussions about accountability, transparency, and moral agency.

In summary, the ethical considerations surrounding wormhole travel are extensive and multifaceted, dancing between the realms of theoretical implications, moral dilemmas, and societal responsibilities. As humanity stands on the precipice of potentially unlocking the mysteries of the cosmos through wormhole technology, the dialogue surrounding ethics must parallel scientific inquiry. Engaging thoughtfully with these complex questions will be essential, as it not only shapes the responsible application of advancements in theoretical physics but also touches our understanding of the very nature of existence, morality, and the human experience within the grand tapestry of the universe. Ultimately, as we delve deeper into the uncharted waters of ethical considerations, our capacity for imagination, wisdom, and responsibility will determine how we navigate the magnificent possibilities that lie ahead.

7.5. The Future of Wormhole Exploration

The potential future of wormhole exploration stands at the precipice of scientific ambition and cultural imagination. With the foundations laid by theoretical physics, tantalizing possibilities related to wormholes evoke profound curiosity about traversing the cosmos and redefining our place in the universe. As research advances and new theoretical frameworks emerge, the impending era of wormhole exploration beckons humanity to engage in a multi-faceted journey characterized not only by technological aspirations but also by cultural reflections and ethical considerations.

One of the most pressing dimensions in the future of wormhole exploration is the continued pursuit of knowledge surrounding the theoretical underpinnings of these enigmatic structures. As physicists and cosmologists probe the intricacies of spacetime, the notion of traversable wormholes becomes a focal point for inquiry. Drawing upon concepts from general relativity and quantum mechanics, researchers push the boundaries of human understanding, seeking pathways that could cement wormholes as practical means of travel rather than mere constructs of imagination. The prospect of traversable wormholes captures the collective consciousness, inspiring scientists and dreamers towards ambitious goals yet to be realized.

In tandem with scientific exploration, the cultural impact of wormholes will undoubtedly flourish in the narrative landscapes of literature, film, and media. As people engage with fantastical representations of wormholes, the idea becomes interwoven with aspirations for cosmic discovery and adventure. This cultural fascination will facilitate discussions about the implications of advanced travel, setting the stage for broader considerations surrounding time, identity, and connectivity as humanity contemplates its destiny beyond the confines of Earth. As new stories emerge, they will continue to shape the public's perception of science, inspiring curiosity about what lies in the depths of the cosmos.

The ethical ramifications of wormhole exploration will remain a pivotal topic as humanity approaches the potential realities of realizing such capabilities. Questions surrounding the morality of altering timelines, intervening in historical events, and the environmental responsibilities toward extraterrestrial worlds will shape the discourse around the development and implementation of wormhole technologies. Engaging in conversations that reconcile scientific ambition with ethical frameworks is essential to ensure that exploration of the unknown does not sacrifice moral responsibilities. As society grapples with these considerations, the dialogue surrounding wormholes will be enriched by deeper insights into humanity's place in the grand tapestry of nature.

The forthcoming era of wormhole exploration also fosters cross-disciplinary collaboration, drawing each domain into a unified endeavor to bridge gaps between physics, philosophy, culture, and technology.

These interdisciplinary dialogues can facilitate innovations in related fields such as robotics, artificial intelligence, and astrobiology. As researchers develop theories and technologies related to wormholes, the creative intersections fostered through collaboration will prompt breakthroughs that propel humanity closer to the threshold of cosmic exploration. Insights gained from one discipline can bolster advancements in others, ultimately creating a holistic approach to understanding the universe.

As aspirations for exploring wormholes extend into the future, the prospect of scientific discovery remains ever-present. Early investigations undertaken by pioneering physicists will lay the groundwork for an array of technological advancements that may one day allow exploration of these cosmic shortcuts. Whether through enhanced simulations, innovative spacecraft designs, or artificial intelligence systems, the unfolding journey promises to unlock previously unimaginable dimensions of scientific understanding. The pursuit of knowledge will transcend generational boundaries, providing a narrative arc that highlights humanity's quest to unravel the mysteries of existence.

Thus, the future of wormhole exploration is not merely an ambitious scientific endeavor; it embodies the aspirations of an entire civilization yearning to connect with the cosmos. As we observe the convergence of scientific inquiry, cultural imagination, and ethical exploration, we find ourselves standing at the threshold of possibility. The unfolding narrative promises to inspire generations of thinkers, creators, and adventurers eager to uncover the mysteries of the universe and chart a path toward a destiny that beckons from beyond the stars.

As we embark on this journey into the unknown, we invite the curious and the imaginative to join us. With each discovery, each story shared, and each ethical consideration faced, we come closer to realizing the extraordinary potential of wormhole exploration—an opportunity to transcend our earthly limitations and explore the vast expanse of existence itself. The future may hold answers to questions we have yet to ask, and the journey of discovery awaits those who dare to step through the cosmic doorway, embracing the infinite possibilities that lie ahead.

8. The Technology of the Future: Simulating and Exploring Wormholes

8.1. Virtual Simulations

Virtual simulations represent a pivotal development in the exploration and understanding of wormholes, providing a means to visualize and analyze these complex theoretical constructs in a controlled and manipulable environment. As scientists grapple with the intricacies involved in wormhole physics, virtual simulations serve as essential tools for studying the properties, behaviors, and implications of these enigmatic structures without the constraints of physical experimentation. This subchapter will explore current efforts in creating virtual models of wormholes, their scientific significance, and their potential applications in future research.

At the core of virtual simulations of wormholes is the use of sophisticated computational models that integrate the principles of general relativity and quantum mechanics. These simulations allow physicists to manipulate variables such as mass, energy density, and the geometry of spacetime, enabling the examination of how different conditions affect the stability and traversability of wormholes. By creating detailed virtual representations, researchers can test specific scenarios that would be challenging or impossible to replicate in the real world, providing invaluable insights into the mechanics of wormhole formation and behavior.

One notable aspect of virtual simulations is their ability to visualize how a wormhole would appear and function. Utilizing advanced graphics and modern computing power, these simulations can depict the swirling geometries that characterize wormholes and illustrate the flow of light and matter around them. By animating the interactions between various forces at play, such as gravitational pull and exotic matter quantities, scientists can observe the potential instability of a wormhole under certain conditions and investigate strategies for maintaining its structural integrity.

Emerging technologies such as virtual reality (VR) and augmented reality (AR) further enhance the possibilities offered by simulations. By creating immersive environments, researchers and educators can engage audiences, enabling them to visualize complex concepts related to wormholes firsthand. These technologies augment traditional approaches to teaching and understanding physics, allowing individuals to interact with three-dimensional models, fostering an intuitive understanding of the intricacies at play.

Furthermore, virtual simulations play a vital role in collaborative research initiatives. Scientists from around the world can share and refine virtual models, pooling their insights and findings to develop more comprehensive understandings of wormhole theory. Simulation platforms can facilitate international collaborations, enabling researchers to assess different approaches and perspectives, thus enhancing the overall discourse surrounding wormholes. As advancements in computational power and algorithms continue to progress, the fidelity and accuracy of these simulations are likely to improve, leading to deeper insights into the behavior and implications of wormholes.

One area of focus within virtual simulations is the examination of traversable wormholes, where researchers analyze the conditions necessary for safe travel and the potential challenges that may arise. By exploring variables such as the amount of exotic matter required to stabilize a traversable wormhole, scientists can assess the feasibility of such structures in practical scenarios. The simulations can shed light on how occupants might experience gravitational forces or radiation exposure during traversal, contributing to our understanding of the implications of wormhole travel for human explorers and advanced technology.

In a broader context, the insights drawn from these virtual simulations can inform real-world experimental designs and hypotheses in related fields such as high-energy physics, astrophysics, and cosmology. By grounding theoretical constructs in visual simulations, researchers can articulate clearer questions for empirical investigations, ultimately speeding up the pace of discovery and innovations related to wormhole technology.

In conclusion, virtual simulations represent a significant step forward in understanding the complexities of wormholes, facilitating exploration that transcends traditional limitations in theoretical physics. By utilizing advanced computational tools, scientists can visualize, analyze, and evaluate the intricate mechanics and implications of wormholes in controlled environments. The continuous advancement of simulation technologies, coupled with collaborative efforts among researchers, ensures that the study of wormholes will not only remain at the cutting edge of theoretical exploration but also inspire future innovations in our quest to understand the mysteries of the cosmos. As we further engage with these simulations, the possibility of unlocking new knowledge about wormholes and their potential for traversing the universe becomes increasingly tangible, reinforcing the power of imagination and inquiry in pushing the frontiers of scientific understanding.

8.2. Spacecraft Design for Wormhole Travel

The design of spacecraft for the purpose of wormhole travel underlines an ambitious intersection of theoretical physics, engineering capabilities, and imaginative speculation. As humanity reaches toward the stars, the challenge of crafting vehicles capable of traversing these theoretical constructs forms a critical piece of the puzzle, marrying bold vision with the complexities of modern science and technology. This discussion delves deeply into the principles and concepts involved in spacecraft design for wormhole travel, highlighting the numerous elements that come together in such an audacious endeavor.

First and foremost, the foundational understanding of wormholes is that they are hypothesized shortcuts through spacetime that could potentially connect distant regions of the universe—or even alter temporal dimensions. For a spacecraft to traverse a wormhole safely, it must be constructed with an acute awareness of the extraordinary gravitational forces, exotic matter requirements, and spacetime fluctuations that characterize these structures. As such, the design process for these hypothetical craft must account for a range of physical and engineering principles to ensure a viable means of travel.

One of the most significant considerations in spacecraft design for wormhole travel involves the material composition and structural integrity of the craft. Given that traversable wormholes may require the presence of exotic matter to stabilize their throats and maintain open connections, the spacecraft must be able to withstand the intense gravitational pressures experienced at the entrance of a wormhole. Advanced materials, potentially inspired by the fields of nanotechnology and metamaterials, may need to be engineered —capable of enduring extreme stress, temperature variations, and radiation. Innovations in nanofabrication could lead to the development of lightweight yet immensely strong materials, lending themselves to the creation of a spacecraft that can handle the rigors of wormhole traversal.

Moreover, the propulsion systems of such spacecraft represent another crucial aspect of their design. Traditional modes of propulsion would likely be inadequate for the quick maneuvering required to approach and effectively enter a wormhole. Instead, innovative propulsion mechanisms, such as those utilizing ion propulsion or theoretical concepts like warp drives, may be explored. These propulsion systems would need to generate the immense energies required to navigate the gravitational complexities of wormhole mouths while maintaining speed and stability. Researchers continue to investigate the principles behind exotic propulsion methods, aiming to harness energies that push the boundaries of contemporary understanding.

The navigation systems crucial for traversing wormholes would require major advancements to ensure that spacecraft can enter and exit these constructs accurately. This involves not only understanding the geometry of spacetime around the wormhole but also needing instruments that can track rapidly changing gravitational fields. High-precision sensors and AI-driven algorithms would be needed to compute the trajectory within the gravity wells and fluctuations inherent in wormhole dynamics. The development of robust onboard systems capable of real-time data analysis would aid in guiding the craft safely through these complex passages.

Furthermore, the design of the spacecraft must prioritize the safety and well-being of its occupants. The human experience of traversing a wormhole raises additional design considerations—including life support systems, radiation shielding, and psychological impacts of potential speed-of-light travel. Provisions for mitigating the effects of extreme acceleration and gravitational forces must be integral aspects of the design. The use of advanced technologies that can ensure not only physical safety but also provide psychological comfort through-out the journey will be crucial for maintaining crew morale during what could be an unprecedented excursion.

Additionally, establishing communication systems capable of func-tioning through wormholes would be essential. Due to the distortions imposed by the curvature of spacetime around a wormhole, ensur-ing continuous communication with base stations or Earth during the voyage becomes a complex challenge. Researchers may need to explore how signals can be sent effectively while accounting for potential delays or disruptions in transmission caused by the unique physics of wormhole travel. Innovative approaches may rely on the-ories related to quantum entanglement or advanced signal processing techniques to establish reliable communication networks.

Finally, the legal and ethical implications of designing spacecraft for wormhole travel are questions that must be integrated into the development process. Principles of responsibility, accountability, and governance over such advanced technologies will require close collaboration with ethicists, legal experts, and regulatory bodies to ensure that exploration is underpinned by a commitment to ethical standards and sustainability. The narrative of exploring wormholes should not only encompass scientific ambition but also consider humanity's interconnectedness and responsibility toward both our home planet and any potentially discovered extraterrestrial environ-ments.

In summary, the design of spacecraft for wormhole travel encapsulates a multifaceted venture that demands rigorous scientific exploration, technological innovation, and ethical reflection. Through interdisciplinary collaboration and a commitment to pushing the frontiers of knowledge, humanity may one day unlock the mysteries of wormholes, transforming dreams of interstellar travel into tangible realities. As researchers and engineers continue to work diligently, the evolution of spacecraft design offers a captivating glimpse into the boundless possibilities awaiting exploration and discovery across the cosmic expanse.

8.3. Potential Impacts on Space Exploration

As humanity stands on the brink of deep space exploration, the potential impacts of wormhole technology could revolutionize the way we traverse the cosmos. The implications of utilizing wormholes, if they were found to be stable and traversable, extend far beyond mere travel; they could redefine our understanding of distance, time, and the very fabric of the universe. Wormholes offer the tantalizing possibility of connecting distant regions of space instantaneously, transforming interstellar travel from a dream into a pragmatic endeavor.

Imagine a future where the vastness of the galaxy—a barrier perceived as insurmountable—becomes navigable in mere moments. With wormholes, the limiting factor of light speed travel fades, allowing humanity to reach previously unreachable star systems. The establishment of a network of wormholes could lead to a new era of exploration and colonization, where ships embark on journeys that once took hundreds or thousands of years, now achievable within hours or days. The complexities of space travel would mitigate dramatically as the arduous challenges associated with long-duration missions—such as resource management and psychological strain on astronauts—could be alleviated through instantaneous transport.

In addition to facilitating exploration, wormhole technology could serve as a catalyst for broader scientific discovery. The ability to rapidly access distant celestial bodies could expedite the study of exoplanets and astrobiology, enabling scientists to gather data and perform experiments on locations harnessing conditions that may foster life. Research on the atmospheres, surface compositions, and potential biosignatures of such worlds could accelerate our quest to answer the profound question of whether we are alone in the universe. Furthermore, as we venture into the depths of space, the encounters with new environments could unveil unknown physics, leading to unexpected discoveries that deepen our understanding of the laws governing the cosmos.

The integration of wormhole technology could also bear significant implications for humanity's resource management. If it becomes feasible to access distant regions of space instantly, the prospect of mining asteroids or harvesting resources from other planetary bodies may no longer remain theoretical. The ability to transport materials back to Earth with ease could alleviate resource scarcity, igniting economic growth while addressing environmental concerns surrounding resource extraction on our home planet. This newfound accessibility could shift our economic landscape, leading to the development of industries predicated on space travel and extraterrestrial resource utilization.

However, the introduction of such revolutionary technology also requires careful consideration of ethical implications and governance. With the potential to access new environments comes the responsibility to protect any ecosystems and civilizations that may exist in those realms. The exploration of wormholes must be coupled with comprehensive policies that prioritize planetary protection and ethical standards for engagement with extraterrestrial life. Collaboration between scientists, policymakers, and ethicists will be essential to establish guidelines that ensure we explore responsibly, without causing harm to new worlds or their inhabitants.

In the context of interstellar communication and networking, wormholes may also enhance humanity's ability to share knowledge and experiences, fostering global collaboration in ways we have yet to idealize. The realization of wormhole technology could enable instantaneous communication across vast distances, negating the time delays associated with traditional methods. This interconnectedness could usher in an age of heightened collaboration, innovation, and shared understanding as scientists and researchers from around the globe work together in real-time to unlock the mysteries of the universe.

In conclusion, the impacts of wormhole technology could stretch far beyond our current understanding of space travel. As we journey into the stars with the potential to traverse the vastness using wormholes, we may redefine the parameters of exploration, resource management, and even our ethical obligations toward the cosmos. The adventure of life among the stars beckons, opening pathways that could profoundly alter our trajectory as a species bound together by knowledge and curiosity. As the dream of wormhole travel evolves from theory to reality, we may just find ourselves on the precipice of a new cosmic era, fueled by the possibilities that lie beyond the known universe.

8.4. The Role of Artificial Intelligence

The role of artificial intelligence (AI) in the context of wormhole research and travel is becoming increasingly crucial, aligning the leaps in computational capabilities with the complexities of theoretical physics. As scientists endeavor to unlock the mysteries surrounding wormholes, AI holds the potential to facilitate research, optimize designs, and simulate intricate scenarios that surpass human cognitive capabilities. By harnessing AI, researchers can navigate the convoluted landscape of wormhole theories, modeling, and practical applications, thereby paving the way for advancements in interstellar travel.

At the heart of AI's contribution to wormhole exploration lies its ability to process vast amounts of data and identify patterns far beyond human analytical capacity. In the field of theoretical physics, where the equations governing wormholes can be incredibly complex, AI algorithms can assist researchers in dissecting these equations and drawing connections between various theoretical frameworks.

Machine learning techniques can be employed to train models that recognize relationships within data sets generated from simulations, historical research outcomes, and experimental results. This capability allows physicists to develop insights into the conditions necessary for stable wormhole formation, optimizing their understanding of how exotic matter and gravitational forces interact within these structures.

AI's role extends beyond theoretical analysis, embracing practical applications in the design and construction of spacecraft capable of traversing wormholes. Through advanced simulations, AI can optimize the architecture of spacecraft, accounting for factors such as structural integrity under extreme conditions, material selection, and propulsion methods. By utilizing generative design algorithms, engineers can explore multiple iterations of spacecraft designs, selecting configurations that best meet the requirements of navigating through the unique gravitational environments associated with wormholes. This optimization process not only enhances the practicality of spacecraft construction but also accelerates the development timeline, potentially propelling wormhole travel from the realm of theoretical speculation into feasible engineering.

Moreover, AI-driven systems have the potential to assist in real-time navigation during wormhole travel. Once a spacecraft approaches a wormhole, the ability to analyze dynamic conditions is paramount. AI can process sensory data rapidly, providing guidance for optimal entry and exit points while calculating trajectories that maximize the safety and efficiency of traversal. These systems could predict shifts in the gravitational field surrounding the wormhole throat, allowing for adaptive navigation strategies that respond to ever-changing conditions. This adaptive capability is particularly essential in the unpredictable gravitational landscape of a wormhole, where slight adjustments can have significant consequences.

The integration of AI in wormhole research also emphasizes collaborative efforts across disciplines. As physicists and computer scientists work in tandem, the development of algorithms tailored for wormhole modeling can lead to breakthroughs in both theoretical understandings and practical adaptations. Interdisciplinary research enables the sharing of knowledge across fields, fostering innovation that benefits both the scientific community and technological advancement.

AI's role in understanding the ethical considerations of wormhole travel shouldn't be overlooked. As advances in technology continue, ethical frameworks surrounding the implications of time travel and exploration must evolve. AI can facilitate discussions about the potential outcomes of wormhole travel, evaluating risks and rewards associated with advancing these technologies into practical application. By assessing various scenarios, AI systems can help researchers envision and navigate the ethical terrain tied to the exploration of time and space, ensuring that scientific ambition remains aligned with moral responsibility.

In conclusion, AI serves as a powerful ally in the quest to understand and utilize wormholes for interstellar travel. By leveraging its capabilities in data analysis, design optimization, navigation, and ethical consideration, the integration of artificial intelligence into wormhole research promises to enhance our understanding of these enigmatic structures while propelling humanity forward into an era of exploration previously confined to the realms of science fiction. As we navigate this journey, the fusion of human ingenuity and artificial intelligence will be essential in realizing the potential of wormhole technology, fostering an exciting future where the cosmos becomes a more accessible frontier.

8.5. The Future of Astrobiology

In the continuously evolving landscape of astrobiology, the concept of wormholes presents a tantalizing avenue for unraveling the mysteries of extraterrestrial life. As our scientific understanding advances, coupled with the burgeoning technological capabilities surrounding theoretical concepts like wormholes, the potential for discovering life beyond our planet expands significantly. This intertwining of wormhole exploration with astrobiological inquiry anticipates a revolutionary shift in how we might approach the search for life in the cosmos.

Wormholes, as theoretical bridges connecting disparate points in spacetime, could potentially facilitate the rapid travel to distant star systems and realms beyond our current reach. Engaging with these constructs allows scientists to ponder how access to remote regions of the universe may yield vital insights into the existence of extraterrestrial ecosystems. Imagine, for instance, a technologically advanced civilization capable of engineering stable wormholes, enabling direct observation of potentially habitable exoplanets located light-years away. This capability would minimize the immense timescales traditionally associated with space travel and exploration, positioning humanity to engage with new worlds more effectively.

From the perspective of astrobiology, the study of exoplanets is already rich with data illustrating varying conditions that could support life. The recent excitement surrounding planets located within the habitable zones of distant stars emphasizes the need for innovative research methodologies conducive to extensive exploration. Access to wormhole travel could significantly enhance our capacity to sample atmospheres, analyze surface conditions, and detect biomarkers indicative of biological activity. Wormhole technology might enable expeditions to undergo rapid sequential encounters with multiple exoplanets previously deemed unreachable, meaning we could gather vast datasets that can inform our understanding of life's potential adaptability across diverse environmental contexts.

Equally crucial is the idea that wormholes might open pathways not only to habitable worlds but also to celestial phenomena that hold key insights into the origins of life itself. The exploration of gas giants, icy moons, or potentially habitable dwarf planets could all yield vital information regarding precursors to life, such as the presence of essential elements, organic compounds, or even subsurface oceans teeming with microbial life. Harnessing wormhole travel could enable astrobiologists to delve into these environments with greater precision, shedding new light on how life might arise, adapt, and evolve under varying cosmic conditions.

Moreover, the scientific collaboration between disciplines—including astrophysics, engineering, and biology—would be essential to the effective utilization of wormhole technology for astrobiological exploration. As scientists work together to build frameworks for understanding these potential pathways, they would enhance our collective knowledge surrounding not only the conditions for life across the universe but also the very nature of life itself. Each exploration through a wormhole could lead to unprecedented discoveries that redefine our parameters for what constitutes living organisms in diverse contexts, amplifying our appreciation for life's resilience and diversity.

While the allure of wormholes is enticing, researchers must remain cognizant of the numerous ethical considerations that come with such a profound capability. Should we discover extraterrestrial life, the ethical implications of engaging with these organisms must take center stage. The responsibilities of protecting potential ecosystems and ensuring that our interference does not disrupt nascent forms of life become critical questions that must be contemplated thoughtfully. The narratives surrounding our exploration of the unknown entangle not only the quest for knowledge but also the moral dimensions that arise from wielding such power.

The future of astrobiology, particularly in the context of wormhole exploration, envisions a world where interstellar travel transforms our quest for understanding life beyond Earth. Wormholes promise to unlock new possibilities, enhancing our ability to reach distant frontiers and engage with different manifestations of life. As we navigate this transformative journey, interdisciplinary collaboration, foresight in ethical implications, and a deep understanding of scientific principles will be crucial as we venture into the cosmic unknown, emboldened by the opportunities that wormholes present. Ultimately, wormhole technology stands poised to deepen our comprehension of existence itself, inviting a more profound appreciation for the enigmatic nature of life across the universe.

9. Case Studies: Exploring the Scientific Research on Wormholes

9.1. Famous Experiments and Theories

Famous experiments and theories surrounding wormholes have emerged as critical components of our understanding of these fascinating phenomena, intertwining the realms of theoretical physics and scientific inquiry. Each contribution builds a broader narrative around the potential existence, stability, and traversability of wormholes, highlighting the collaborative spirit of physicists and mathematicians dedicated to exploring the intricacies of the universe.

The theoretical foundation for wormholes begins with the implications of Albert Einstein's general relativity, introduced in 1915. Einstein's equations revealed how gravitational forces could warp the fabric of spacetime, leading to the first ideas of tunnels connecting distant points in the cosmos. In 1935, Einstein, alongside Nathan Rosen, proposed a specific solution to these equations, presenting what is now recognized as the Einstein-Rosen Bridge. Although initially viewed as a mathematical curiosity, this work laid the groundwork for deeper explorations into the nature of wormholes.

One of the significant avenues of contemporary research involves the models of traversable wormholes proposed by physicist Kip Thorne and his colleagues in the late 1980s. They suggested that wormholes could be stabilized with exotic matter—hypothetical substances exhibiting negative energy density. This led to a series of theoretical explorations around the conditions required to maintain a stable wormhole and the implications for time travel. The work of Thorne and others earned a place within popular culture, clearly illustrated in films such as "Interstellar," where his scientific contributions lent authenticity to the narrative's depiction of traveling through a wormhole.

Another influential theoretical model stems from the investigation of wormholes within the context of quantum mechanics. Quantum theories suggest that micro-wormholes may exist momentarily, conceived as spontaneous fluctuations in the fabric of spacetime. These fleeting structures kindle excitement about the potential connection between quantum mechanics and the macroscopic adventures of wormhole travel. Exploring how quantum realities might yield insights into themes traditionally reserved for science fiction further challenges the boundaries of our understanding.

Experimental endeavors have also sought to develop testing frameworks for the fundamental ideas surrounding wormholes. While direct manipulation of these cosmic structures remains beyond current technological capabilities, researchers have explored related phenomena, such as gravitational waves, as key signals linked to the cosmic fabric affected by exotic configurations akin to wormholes. The detection of gravitational waves provides opportunities for laboratory environments to simulate conditions that might resemble those anticipated around wormholes, creating enriched dialogues between theory and empirical data.

Collaborative efforts in research laboratories worldwide exemplify the synergy between mathematical theorists and experimental physicists, producing a dynamic discourse around wormholes and their implications. Institutions across the globe have worked collaboratively to explore the gated pathways to understanding wormholes, pairing cutting-edge computational modeling with experimental designs that can gauge the properties of spacetime.

Despite the rigorous pursuit of formal research over decades, the journey is marked by trials and challenges within the scientific community. Wormhole theories often evoke skepticism rooted in the speculative nature of the concepts themselves, requiring investigators to navigate debates about stability and traversability. Key hurdles remain surrounding the practical realization of exotic matter and the methods by which physicists might create or observe these structures. Whilel significant breakthroughs remain elusive, researchers remain undeterred. Each inquiry represents an opportunity to deepen understanding, strengthening the collective pursuit of knowledge.

As insights into wormhole research unfold, moments of breakthrough emerge as noteworthy milestones. Discoveries about space-time geometry and alterations influenced by mass and energy continue to rewrite scientific paradigms surrounding our cosmos. The pursuit to understand black holes, event horizons, and related cosmic phenomena invariably circles back to the exploratory thread of wormholes—a tantalizing glimpse of what lies beyond conventional frameworks.

In conclusion, examining the significant experiments and theories surrounding wormholes reveals the interconnected web of human curiosity, scientific ambition, and theoretical exploration. As physicists collectively strive to address the versatility and implications of these cosmic constructs, their work enhances our understanding of the universe's complex tapestry. Each advancement invites curiosity and imagination, opening doors towards potential realities where wormholes might become tangible pathways through the ever-enigmatic expanse of spacetime. Ultimately, this convergence of inquiry enhances our aspirations for exploration as humanity gazes up toward the cosmos, yearning for connections that transcend conventional limits.

9.2. Collaborative Efforts Worldwide

Around the globe, scientists and researchers are engaging in collaborative efforts to deepen our understanding of wormholes, a scientific frontier that merges advanced physics with the tantalizing realms of theoretical possibility. This collaboration bridges academic institutions, fosters interdisciplinary dialogue, and invites participation from diverse scientific communities, all united by the aspiration to unlock the mysteries of the universe.

One prominent example of international cooperation in this realm is the Interstellar Probe Initiative, which brings together physicists, engineers, and astronomers from multiple countries to investigate the viability of traveling through wormholes. This initiative aims to consolidate resources and expertise, creating a comprehensive research network that can tackle the multifarious challenges associated with wormhole physics. By pooling knowledge from various cultures, languages, and ideas, participating institutions attain insights that would be unachievable in isolation.

In addition to formal initiatives, numerous conferences and workshops dedicated to the study of wormholes facilitate discussion and collaboration among leading experts in the field. These gatherings create fertile ground for sharing breakthroughs and theoretical advancements while empowering junior researchers and students to contribute fresh perspectives. Such forums not only kindle scientific friendships but also set the stage for collaborative publications and joint projects, further amplifying the global dialogue surrounding wormhole research.

Moreover, collaborative efforts have led to significant advancements in computational modeling techniques. Researchers from different institutions often share their algorithms and simulation software, refining methodologies to simulate the dynamics of wormholes accurately. This cooperation enhances the precision of models that predict how wormholes might interact with other astrophysical phenomena, pushing the boundaries of contemporary understanding in profound ways.

As the scientific community investigates the practical considerations surrounding wormholes, interdisciplinary partnerships with engineering departments and private industry have begun to emerge. These partnerships explore the technological ramifications of wormhole research, focusing on potential advances in materials science or propulsion technology that may be required to fabricate vehicles for traversing wormholes. By fostering collaboration between theoretical physicists, engineers, and entrepreneurs, these multifaceted partnerships cultivate a vibrant ecosystem that bridges theoretical inquiry with practical innovation.

Funding institutions and government agencies are increasingly recognizing the value of supporting collaborative research efforts focused on wormholes. Grants aimed at interdisciplinary programs encourage teams to confront the complexities of wormhole physics holistically. Whether addressing the foundational principles behind their existence or exploring the engineering challenges related to their utilization, collaborative funding recognizes the necessity of collective expertise. This commitment ensures the continuation of exploratory research that pushes the thresholds of our understanding.

Furthermore, the powerful synergy that emerges from these collaborative efforts often inspires innovative educational initiatives. Outreach programs aimed at engaging high school and university students in wormhole research can inspire the next generation of physicists. For instance, summer camps or workshops can blend theoretical teachings with hands-on activities demonstrating aspects of wormhole science, thus awakening curiosity in young minds. These educational attempts fuel the aspirations of future researchers who may one day make groundbreaking discoveries in the field.

In sum, the collaborative efforts unfolding worldwide represent a dynamic and transformative force in the quest to understand wormholes. By forging connections across institutions, disciplines, and cultures, scientists are collectively tackling the enigmas posed by these cosmic phenomena, cultivating a richer narrative surrounding potential cosmic journeys. It is through these collaborative endeavors that the frontiers of science advance, bringing humanity closer to revealing the secrets of the cosmos and confronting the incredible possibilities that lie within it. Ultimately, as efforts continue to coalesce around the pursuit of wormholes, we are reminded of the power of collaborative inquiry to inspire innovation, challenge existing paradigms, and ignite the imaginations of all who gaze into the vastness of the universe.

9.3. Institutional Research and Funding

Institutional research and funding play a pivotal role in advancing the study of wormholes, an area at the intersection of theoretical physics and cosmology that intrigues both scientists and the public alike. As the pursuit of understanding wormholes and their implications for time travel and interstellar exploration unfolds, the importance of financial backing and institutional support cannot be overstated.

One of the primary sources of funding for wormhole research comes from governmental space agencies such as NASA and the European Space Agency (ESA). These organizations have recognized the potential of advanced theories in physics to not only expand our understanding of the universe but also to inspire technological advancements that can benefit humanity. By investing in research programs that delve into the complexities of wormholes, these agencies aim to cultivate new scientific knowledge that could ultimately inform future explorations into deep space.

In addition to governmental funding, academic institutions and private research foundations contribute significantly to wormhole research. Universities with strong physics departments frequently establish grants to encourage research into general relativity, quantum mechanics, and their applications to wormhole theories. Interdisciplinary collaborations within academic settings, involving physicists, mathematicians, and engineers, can often lead to innovative research initiatives that push the boundaries of our understanding. Projects such as these benefit from the support of institutional funding that encourages creative exploration while providing the resources necessary to conduct comprehensive research.

Moreover, private sector investments are increasingly supporting wormhole research through partnerships with academic institutions and national laboratories. Technology firms interested in leveraging advances in theoretical physics to enhance computational power or develop novel materials have begun to back research projects focused on wormholes. These collaborative efforts can lead to exciting innovations that transcend the academic realm and have real-world applications. By aligning research perspectives with technological advancements, such partnerships illustrate how interdisciplinary cooperation can propel the field of wormhole research forward.

Crunching numbers or developing theoretical frameworks is rarely sufficient on its own; outreach and public engagement also play an essential role in garnering support for wormhole research. Public interest in astrophysics and the broader potential implications of wormhole technology can elevate funding priorities. Science communicators, educational outreach programs, and popular media narratives that highlight the beauty and mystery of wormholes are invaluable in fostering excitement and engagement among the public. This increased enthusiasm can translate to greater political and financial support, further legitimizing the scientific pursuit of these phenomena.

The importance of funding in wormhole research goes beyond mere support for projects; it cultivates the environment necessary for breakthroughs and transformative discoveries. The dream of harnessing wormhole technology reflects an ambition that stretches across disciplines and generations. The cultivation of financial resources enables the recruitment of minds passionate about physics, encourages the development of experimental designs, and ultimately positions researchers to confront the scientific challenges that remain.

In conclusion, institutional research and funding are critical to advancing the frontier of wormhole science. The convergence of governmental support, academic initiatives, private investments, and public engagement creates an ecosystem conducive to exploration and discovery. As financial backing continues to elevate the importance of wormhole studies, the scientific community inches closer to unraveling the mysteries of these cosmic structures, fueling aspirations for the future of space travel and our understanding of the universe's fabric. The ongoing pursuit of wormholes embodies humanity's relentless quest to transcend limitations and explore the boundless possibilities that await beyond the stars.

9.4. Failures and Successes

The quest to understand wormholes has been marked by both remarkable successes and notable failures that underscore the challenges inherent to such advanced theoretical constructs. As researchers dive into the mysteries of these cosmic bridges, they often navigate the delicate balance between ambitious aspirations and the pragmatic realities of scientific inquiry.

Failures in the pursuit of wormhole research often stem from the profound complexity of the concepts involved. Initial explorations into the theoretical frameworks of wormholes, such as those formulated by Einstein and Rosen, faced immediate criticism for lacking empirical evidence or practical application. Although their work laid a critical foundation, it quickly became apparent that simply deriving elegant mathematical models was insufficient to draw concrete conclusions about the existence or viability of traversable wormholes. This call for empirical validation highlighted the gap between theory and real-world observation—a challenge that has persisted throughout the realm of theoretical physics.

As researchers endeavored to pursue the idea of creating traversable wormholes, the requirement for exotic matter presented significant setbacks. This hypothetical substance, necessary for stabilizing wormhole throats and allowing for safe travel, has remained elusive. Multiple attempts to incorporate aspects of exotic matter into existing theories have led to extensive speculation but little tangible advancement. Theoretical constructs surrounding wormhole stability often incorporate exotic matter as a crux component, yet the inability to observe or produce it experimentally has hindered progress. This has resulted in scientific frustration, as teams grapple with the chasm between theoretical predictions and practical realizations.

However, not all has been in vain—through the labyrinth of challenges have emerged notable successes that have shed light on the nature of wormholes and bolstered the ongoing inquiry. Landmark achievements include successful collaborations across disciplines, ultimately leading to deeper insights into fundamental aspects of general relativity and quantum mechanics. The emergence of gravitational wave detection as a practical reality has represented a triumph for the scientific community, signaling a new method for observing phenomena predicted by these theoretical frameworks. Such observations pave the way for heightened understanding of spacetime anomalies, potentially even leading to confirmation of wormhole-like structures in the cosmos.

Additionally, the advancements in simulations and computational modeling have marked significant successes in the field. By utilizing powerful computing systems to create detailed visualizations and analyses of wormhole dynamics, researchers can explore scenarios previously relegated to the realms of speculation. These virtual models allow for the manipulation and observation of known variables in controlled environments, enabling scientists to hypothesize about the behaviors and characteristics of wormholes as they relate to complex gravitational interactions. These advancements have not only enriched our understanding of wormholes themselves, but they have also provided broader methodologies in theoretical physics that extend well beyond this singular focus.

Moreover, interdisciplinary collaborative efforts represent an incremental success in merging theoretical constructs with practical applications. The blending of perspectives from theoretical physicists, engineers, and computer scientists has catalyzed innovations in research methods that engage new avenues of exploration. These partnerships illustrate how the complexities surrounding wormholes invite wider engagement across fields, generating ongoing dialogues that foster fresh insights and innovative solutions.

As scientists continue to pursue the intricacies of wormhole travel, the interplay between failures and successes will undoubtedly shape the trajectory of this research. Each setback, rather than serving merely as a deterrent, propels the scientific inquiry forward, inspiring resilience and adaptability. The continued exploration of these cosmic constructs highlights humanity's relentless curiosity; the ambition to delve into the unknown persists despite the complexities and demands of modern scientific pursuits.

In conclusion, the narrative of wormhole research serves as a testament to the nature of scientific inquiry: a journey marked by both trials and triumphs. As physicists and astronomers build upon their foundational understanding, the intricate dance between failure and success will continue to inspire the quest for knowledge and innovation within the realms of wormholes, challenging the boundaries of human understanding and exploration of the cosmos.

9.5. Breakthrough Discoveries

The prospect of breakthrough discoveries in the realm of wormhole research embodies a captivating blend of theoretical advancements and groundbreaking insights that challenge our understanding of the universe. These moments, often emerging from rigorous scientific inquiry and bold speculation, pave the way for new paradigms in physics, altering perceptions about time, space, and the fundamental structure of reality itself.

One of the most significant breakthrough discoveries occurred in the late 20th century when Kip Thorne and his colleagues explored the concept of traversable wormholes. Their 1988 paper shifted the discussion by introducing the idea that these cosmic bridges could theoretically allow for safe travel, drawing on the need for exotic matter to maintain their stability. This pivotal moment captured the attention of both scientists and science fiction writers, propelling wormholes into popular culture while also sparking renewed interest in the study of general relativity and its implications for the cosmos.

Beyond theoretical frameworks, breakthroughs have arisen from the intersection of quantum mechanics and wormhole research. Advances in understanding quantum fluctuations have led to the proposition that micro-wormholes may spontaneously appear and disappear at incredibly small scales. This revelation hints at the potential for hidden structures woven into the fabric of spacetime, challenging traditional notions of continuity and stability. As physicists dive deeper into the implications of quantum mechanics, they unveil new paths for exploration, lending further credibility to the notion that wormholes could be more than mere mathematical abstractions.

Moreover, experimental endeavors that aim to detect gravitational waves have further solidified the connection between observable phenomena and wormhole theory. The landmark discoveries made by the LIGO (Laser Interferometer Gravitational-Wave Observatory) collaboration in 2015 provided empirical evidence of waves originating from massive astronomical events such as black hole mergers. This breakthrough not only revolutionized our understanding of the universe but also reinforced the idea that spacetime is far more dynamic than previously thought. As researchers investigate the signatures of gravitational waves, they may stumble upon clues that illuminate the properties of wormholes or anomalies indicative of their presence.

The role of collaborative research in unveiling breakthrough discoveries cannot be overstated. Initiatives that bring together physicists, mathematicians, and engineers from diverse fields toward a common goal foster an environment ripe for innovation. An example of such collaboration is the European Organization for Nuclear Research (CERN), which supports studies into high-energy physics while also hosting interdisciplinary research. These fertile grounds enable scientists to explore the parameters around wormhole theories, effectively advancing the frontier of knowledge.

Emerging technologies have also facilitated discoveries in wormhole research. The rise of supercomputing and advanced simulation techniques has allowed scientists to model intricate scenarios that provide deeper insights into wormhole behavior, stability, and potential applications. Enhanced data analysis techniques driven by machine learning assist researchers in sifting through vast datasets to identify patterns and correlations that might otherwise remain hidden. These breakthroughs demonstrate the value of embracing new tools and methodologies in the pursuit of understanding complex phenomena.

As this dialogue around wormholes continues, the cultural landscape has significantly influenced the direction of scientific inquiry, igniting public interest and curiosity about the nature of existence. Breakthrough insights permeate popular literature, cinema, and media narratives, creating a compelling synergy that propels both scientists and enthusiasts to engage with these cosmic concepts. The public's fascination with the mysteries of wormholes creates a supportive backdrop for ongoing research, shaping funding priorities and inspiring new generations of scientists in their pursuit of knowledge.

In conclusion, the journey of breakthrough discoveries in wormhole research exemplifies the dynamic and interconnected nature of scientific inquiry. From foundational theories to revolutionary experimental findings, each significant insight builds upon the preceding work of researchers dedicated to exploring the mysteries of the universe. The discoveries surrounding wormholes not only enhance our comprehension of spacetime but also fuel the imagination, inviting questions about the broader implications of traversable pathways through the cosmos. As physicists and dreamers alike continue to examine these enigmatic structures, the anticipation of future breakthroughs encourages humanity to reach for the stars, ever seeking to uncover the profound wonders that lie just beyond our understanding.

10. Physics of an Alternate Universe: Beyond Scientific Paradigms

10.1. Alternate Universes Theories

In the conception of alternate universes, a captivating interplay emerges between theoretical physics and philosophical musings, particularly in regards to wormholes. The notion of alternate universes, often encapsulated within the broader framework of multiverse theories, suggests the presence of numerous, perhaps infinite, parallel realities. These realities could manifest with variations in physical laws, historical events, or even the fundamental nature of existence itself. The exploration of such concepts raises profound implications regarding the nature of wormholes, which could function as conduits between these parallel dimensions and facilitate travel across divergent realities.

Multiverse theories propose various models, some rooted in quantum mechanics, others in cosmological principles. For instance, the Many-Worlds Interpretation of quantum mechanics suggests that every quantum event spawns a branching universe, resulting in alternate realities for every feasible outcome. If wormholes exist, they might serve as theoretical bridges, allowing entities to traverse from one universe to another. Exploring the implications of such travel affords a deeper understanding of reality and existence—one where the consequences of actions in one universe might reverberate into adjacent ones, leading to expansive narratives that challenge our current comprehension of causality.

Within the realm of theoretical astrophysics, the implications of alternate universe physics for wormhole science extend beyond mere speculation. Theoretical frameworks positing the existence of stable, traversable wormholes could necessitate the integration of principles underlying multiverse interactions. Interconnecting these theories may inspire new avenues of research focused on the geometric properties of spacetime structures shaped by multiple universes. Investigative models may delineate configurations that facilitate travel between these dimensions, while also addressing the overarching questions surrounding stability, endurance, and energy requirements for such routes.

Moreover, the role of experimental astroparticle physics becomes pivotal in our exploration of alternate universes connected by wormholes. Investigations into cosmic particles that traverse the universe might yield insights into the very nature of spacetime and its behavior under extreme conditions. By examining cosmic rays or particles emanating from high-energy astrophysical events, scientists may glean valuable information that could bolster the case for or against the existence of wormholes as pathways to alternate realities. The search for anomalies in cosmic data could serve as tangible conduits for validating the theories surrounding multiverses and their interconnectivity through wormholes.

The quest for knowledge surrounding alternate universes and their relation to wormholes also invites us to venture beyond the standard model of particle physics. In this pursuit, researchers explore new possibilities that redefine our understanding of the fundamental forces shaping the universe. By probing phenomena such as dark matter, dark energy, and quantum gravity, scientists can investigate how these constructs connect to the existence of wormholes and their potential inter-universal travel. Expanding the parameters of inquiry may yield groundbreaking discoveries that challenge established paradigms and pave the path toward a richer understanding of the cosmos.

As breakthroughs emerge, the possibilities grow both exhilarating and daunting. The confluence of evidence and speculation around wormholes and alternate universes encourages ongoing dialogue within scientific and philosophical communities. Unearthed anomalies and insights gleaned from experimental ventures may support existing hypotheses or suggest alternate perspectives that redefine our understanding of the intricate web of reality. Each inquiry into these mysteries lends texture to the narrative surrounding existence and opens pathways for deeper exploration of life beyond our known universe.

In summary, the exploration of alternate universes theories invites significant discourse surrounding wormholes as bridges to parallel realities. By delving into the complexities of multiverse physics and the potential interconnections offered by wormholes, researchers stand at the frontier of understanding the multilayered fabric of existence itself. As our quest for knowledge continues and discoveries unfold, the interplay between theoretical inquiry and imaginative exploration will enrich the tapestry of human curiosity, forging ahead into the enigmatic realms of possibility that lie just beyond our current understanding.

10.2. The Role of Theoretical Astrophysics

The role of theoretical astrophysics in the study of wormholes goes beyond mere academic inquiry; it serves as a vital bridge between abstract mathematical models and the tangible possibilities of understanding our universe. The implications of wormholes touch on fundamental questions about the nature of spacetime, the structure of the cosmos, and even the potential for interstellar travel. By delving into mathematical theories, researchers engage with the complex relationships between mass, energy, and gravitational forces that dictate the behavior of such cosmic phenomena.

Theoretical astrophysics provides the mathematical framework that underpins the concept of wormholes. General relativity, as formulated by Albert Einstein, lays the groundwork for understanding how massive objects distort the fabric of spacetime, creating the conditions necessary for wormholes to potentially exist. Researchers utilize equations and geometric models to hypothesize how wormholes might be formed and sustained, contemplating questions of traversability and the role of exotic matter. Such theoretical explorations not only deepen our understanding of gravity and general relativity but also highlight the intricate relationships between spacetime geometry and the potential for interconnectivity across the cosmos.

Moreover, theoretical astrophysics facilitates the exploration of quantum mechanics—the second pillar of modern physics—which provides insights into the potential existence of micro-wormholes resulting from quantum fluctuations. These brief, transient structures prompt significant questions about the nature of reality and the interconnectedness of spacetime. Researchers integrate both frameworks, proposing multiverse theories wherein wormholes act as bridges connecting alternate realities. Theoretical physicists are tasked with developing models that capture the geometry of these hypothetical connections, enabling studies into how matter and energy may interact across universes.

As theoretical frameworks evolve, they also give rise to experimental inquiries. Theoretical astrophysics sparks curiosity about what evidence could validate or nullify the existence of wormholes in reality. This interplay compels researchers to design experiments aimed at probing the fabric of spacetime, seeking anomalies that could hint at the presence of wormhole-like structures or the behavior of particles influenced by such configurations. Observations of gravitational waves or cosmic radiation might yield essential data, guiding our understanding of the conditions necessary to create and sustain stable wormholes.

In addition to guiding experimental approaches, theoretical physics contextualizes the implications of wormholes for future space exploration. The practical applications of wormhole theory could revolutionize our approach to interstellar travel and redefine our understanding of distance and time. By integrating principles of astrophysics with advances in engineering, researchers may outline the requirements for constructing spacecraft capable of traversing these theoretical pathways. The pursuit of theoretical explorations in this context serves as a touchstone for innovation, enabling a shift in focus from mere speculation to actionable inquiry into human exploration of the cosmos.

The implications of wormhole research also extend into broader philosophical conversations about existence, determinism, and free will. Theoretical astrophysics invites reflections on the nature of our reality and the impact of traversing alternate dimensions. If wormholes allow for travel between different timelines, it induces meaningful questions regarding the impact of individual actions, the fluidity of the past, present, and future, and the overall nature of consciousness itself.

In conclusion, the role of theoretical astrophysics in the study of wormholes represents a goldmine of interdisciplinary inquiry, weaving together mathematics, empirical research, engineering, and philosophy. Through rigorous exploration of these concepts, scientists are positioned not only to deepen our understanding of the cosmos but also to open pathways to realizing the possibilities of wormhole travel. As we continue to unravel these theoretical constructs, we stand at a precipice, gazing into the vast unknown of the universe, driven by our insatiable curiosity to explore, discover, and connect.

10.3. Experimental Astroparticle Physics

In the realm of astroparticle physics, the intersection of experimentation and theoretical exploration plays a pivotal role in expanding our understanding of wormholes and their potential implications for the cosmos. This subchapter will delve into the significant contributions of experimental astroparticle physics, focusing on the ways in which cosmic particle studies provide insights that may illuminate the mysteries surrounding these speculative structures.

Astroparticle physics is a multidisciplinary field that examines the fundamental particles of the universe, combining aspects of particle physics, astrophysics, and cosmology. It addresses the profound questions of the universe's origins, composition, and the governing forces that dictate its behavior. Within this framework, researchers study cosmic rays, neutrinos, and dark matter particles, among others. These cosmic entities hold critical clues regarding the nature of spacetime and the potential existence of wormholes.

One of the most exciting avenues of research involves the examination of cosmic rays—high-energy particles originating from outer space that can travel vast distances before colliding with Earth's atmosphere. Scientists employ advanced detectors to analyze these cosmic particles, seeking anomalies that might suggest interactions with exotic matter or fluctuations in spacetime associated with wormhole-like phenomena. Cosmic ray studies can serve as indirect evidence for the existence of wormholes, revealing signatures that challenge or reinforce prevailing theories surrounding their stability and traversability.

Neutrinos, another focal point of experimental astroparticle physics, offer tantalizing possibilities for probing the foundations of wormhole theories. These nearly massless particles interact weakly with matter, allowing them to traverse the universe predominantly unimpeded. The study of neutrinos from high-energy cosmic events, such as supernovae, provides insights into the conditions prevalent in extreme cosmic environments. Analyzing how neutrinos behave in these contexts could yield valuable data regarding the structure of spacetime and potential gateways formed by wormholes.

Moreover, dark matter research holds significant implications for understanding wormhole mechanics. This elusive component constitutes a substantial portion of the universe's mass, yet its nature remains largely unknown. Investigating the behaviors and interactions of dark matter particles may reveal critical information about how mass influences spacetime curvature, possibly yielding insights into how wormholes could stabilize and function. If dark matter portals or wormholic structures can be modeled or identified through experimental investigation, it will deepen our grasp of the universe's complexities.

Furthermore, experimental facilities such as the Large Hadron Collider (LHC) play an integral role in probing beyond the Standard Model of particle physics, effectively expanding the search for exotic matter—an essential element in the theoretical exploration of traversable wormholes. The LHC's experiments provide a platform to observe high-energy collisions, potentially generating conditions conducive to creating transient exotic matter states. Any evidence supporting the existence of such matter would directly bolster the theoretical frameworks surrounding wormhole stability.

Additionally, gravitational wave observatories contribute to our understanding of the spacetime fabric, offering an avenue to examine how colossal cosmic events might correlate with wormhole constructs. Similar to how cosmic rays provide indirect evidence related to wormholes, gravitational wave detections from merging black holes could unveil temporal or spatial anomalies that hint at the overlapping realities wormholes might represent.

In summary, experimental astroparticle physics serves as an essential avenue of inquiry into the complexities surrounding wormholes. Through cosmic particle studies, researchers uncover hints and anomalies that may affirm or question our understanding of these theoretical constructs. As the field continues to advance, the pursuit of insights gleaned from cosmic rays, neutrinos, dark matter, and gravitational waves will enhance our grasp of not just wormholes but also the fundamental principles governing the universe itself. The collaboration between experimentation and theory exemplifies the dynamic nature of scientific exploration, highlighting how insights gained today may illuminate the pathways toward groundbreaking discoveries tomorrow in the quest for understanding the cosmos.

10.4. Beyond the Standard Model

The concept of exploring realms beyond our established scientific paradigms, particularly through the lens of wormhole theory, invites a profound inquiry into what lies ahead in the fabric of the universe. Understanding wormholes fundamentally alters our cosmological perspectives, urging us to bridge the gap between theoretical possibilities and scientific exploration. This journey is not merely a voyage through spacetime but an odyssey that evokes the interconnectedness of science, philosophy, and human aspiration.

Wormholes, as proposed, serve as shortcuts through the tapestry of spacetime, presenting the tantalizing possibility of interstellar travel that could reframe our understanding of distance and time itself.

The implications of verifying the existence of such constructs invite us to reassess our existing scientific frameworks, including the established parameters of general relativity and quantum mechanics. As researchers delve into the intricacies of wormhole stability, exotic matter, and the potential for traversability, they stand at the crossroads of traditional physics and emerging theories that challenge established dogmas.

In this exploratory landscape, various theoretical frameworks have emerged, suggesting the existence of structures that could connect not just distant points in space but even alternate dimensions or parallel universes. This notion of multiverse principles posits thrilling questions about our understanding of reality and existence itself. By extending the dialogue around wormholes to encompass such theories, we open avenues for meaningful discourse about the implications of traversing through different layers of reality.

Collaborative efforts across institutions fuel progress in wormhole research. By pooling resources, knowledge, and diverse perspectives, scientists create a collective intelligence that enriches our investigation into the cosmos's fabric. This collaboration fosters interdisciplinary methodologies, enabling the fusion of theoretical advancements with practical inquiries that may one day yield tangible pathways for space exploration. The integration of theoretical astrophysics with experimental techniques not only enhances our understanding of wormholes but also solidifies the connection between knowledge and societal expectations.

The role of artificial intelligence in facilitating research into wormholes cannot be overlooked. From computational modeling to real-time navigation during potential wormhole travel, AI serves as a powerful ally in the quest for understanding the intricacies of these cosmic constructs. By harnessing AI's capabilities, researchers can investigate scenarios that challenge human cognition, optimizing approaches that may accelerate advancements while adhering to ethical responsibilities.

As we ponder the future implications of wormhole technology, a myriad of possibilities unfolds before us. The potential for instant interstellar travel could revolutionize not just exploration but economic frameworks, resource management, and our fundamental understanding of existence. The ethical dimensions of such capabilities are paramount; ensuring the responsible exploration of alien worlds must remain at the forefront of our endeavors.

Ultimately, this journey reflects humanity's relentless desire to explore the unknown, transcending conventional boundaries to reach for the stars. As we continue to unravel the mysteries of the universe—and the role wormholes may play in shaping our destinies —we stand at an extraordinary juncture, where the lines between science and imagination converge. The quest for knowledge about wormholes beckons us to embrace the infinite possibilities that lie ahead, inviting generations of dreamers and thinkers to embark on an adventure that spans the cosmos. In the grand tapestry of existence, the pursuit of wormhole travel symbolizes the hope, ambition, and creativity that define humanity's legacy among the stars, solidifying our position as explorers of both time and space. The journey continues, inviting us all to imagine, investigate, and intertwine with the vast enigma that is the universe.

10.5. Anomalies and Insights

The study of wormholes has not only provided an exciting avenue in theoretical physics but has also yielded a wealth of anomalies and insights that challenge our current understanding of the universe. As research continues to evolve, unexpected data and experimental observations often lead to breakthrough discoveries that reshape our perception of reality, inviting both skepticism and curiosity among scientists and philosophers alike.

The search for empirical evidence of wormholes is fraught with complexities, and researchers have encountered various anomalies that give rise to intriguing questions. For instance, investigations into the behavior of gravitational waves have sometimes unveiled signatures that hint at the potential presence of wormholes, leading scientists to explore whether these fluctuations could be indicative of collapsing or forming structures at the edges of spacetime. The implications of such findings could lend credence to the existence of wormholes, igniting further inquiries into their stability and traversability.

Moreover, experimental data from high-energy particle collisions in facilities like the Large Hadron Collider (LHC) have occasionally yielded unexpected results. Researchers meticulously analyze the outcomes of these collisions, seeking to uncover anomalies that may suggest the presence of miniature wormhole-like phenomena or transitions between different dimensional states. Instances where predicted particle behaviors deviate from established norms prompt excitement within the scientific community, as they may serve as gateways to understanding the subtleties of wormholes and exotic matter.

Conversely, some data challenge existing theories regarding wormholes, necessitating critical evaluation of the underlying assumptions in current models. For example, attempts to derive consistent and coherent equations describing the stability of traversable wormholes often encounter contradictions that cannot be reconciled within the framework of classical physics. These failures signal a need to revisit fundamental assumptions and explore alternate approaches, invigorating discussions that may eventually lead to novel theoretical paradigms.

Wormhole research has also catalyzed insights into the fundamental nature of spacetime itself. Quantum gravitation theories that emerge from these explorations suggest that spacetime is not simply a static backdrop but a dynamic entity capable of exhibiting anomalies that can complicate classical predictions. Such insights invite reconsideration of accepted scientific paradigms, always pushing the boundary of our understanding.

Furthermore, as discussions around wormholes penetrate into public consciousness, a broader cultural perspective emerges regarding humanity's relationship with knowledge and exploration. The anomalies found in scientific research beckon the curious to question established narratives and consider what lies at the periphery of discovery. The implications of such engagement extend beyond the academic realm, reverberating through wider societal discourse on science, ethics, and the future of exploration.

In conclusion, the realm of anomalies and insights in wormhole research encapsulates the spirit of scientific inquiry—one driven by curiosity, resilience, and the thirst for understanding. As researchers continue to probe the complexities of wormholes, navigating uncharted territories, they not only fortify the foundations of theoretical physics but also evoke broader reflections on existence itself. The journey ahead remains ripe with possibilities, underpinned by the understanding that anomalies may sometimes herald breakthroughs, illuminating the path toward deeper exploration of the cosmos. Embracing the unknown, scientists champion the quest to unlock the secrets of wormholes, culling invaluable truths about our universe and the nature of reality.

11. Practical Implications and Future Prospects

11.1. Implications for Humanity

The concept of wormholes extends far beyond mere scientific curiosity, encompassing profound implications for humanity that touch on our understanding of existence, identity, and our place within the cosmos. Should we be able to harness the reality of wormhole travel, it could mark a monumental leap in human civilization, shaping the very fabric of our social, economic, and cultural landscapes.

Firstly, the realization of stable wormhole technology would fundamentally transform our approach to space exploration. Traditional methods of traversing vast cosmic distances often span lifetimes, impeding our ambitions to engage with the universe. The ability to navigate through wormholes would permit instant travel to far-flung stellar systems, unlocking new frontiers of knowledge about the universe and potentially bringing humanity into contact with extraterrestrial life. This capability could kindle a renaissance of exploration, reminiscent of the great voyages of discovery throughout human history, prompting not only a renewed sense of adventure but also an urgent sense of responsibility as we encounter the unknown.

The implications for science and technology are equally staggering. Beyond simply reaching distant worlds, wormhole travel could facilitate unprecedented scientific research. Imagine the capacity to transport entire laboratories to locations where the mysteries of cosmic phenomena—such as supernovae or black holes—remain elusive. The capacity to conduct experiments in situ or to rapidly sample materials from nascent worlds would revolutionize our understanding of astrophysics and chemistry, leading to advancements that expand the horizons of current scientific inquiry.

The interconnections of humanity's future with wormhole technology also find resonance in economic possibilities. The development of wormhole travel may birth entirely new industries dedicated to space commerce, tourism, and research. The economic implications could redefine our global economy, creating unprecedented opportunities for trade and innovation as new resources and knowledge are accessible. Investment in wormhole technology may attract significant funding from governments, private sectors, and philanthropists, fostering an ecosystem ripe for technological advancements, resource acquisition, and the eventual colonization of distant worlds.

As we analyze the implications for humanity, it is essential to recognize the ethical dimensions entwined with this exploration. With newfound capabilities come responsibilities; the potential to access alternate dimensions or histories raises profound questions about human accountability. Ethical frameworks must guide interactions with newly discovered ecosystems, ensuring that our pursuits do not infringe upon the integrity of these environments or the lives they may harbor. Our quest to explore the unknown must be accompanied by cautious and thoughtful engagement with the potential consequences of our actions.

Moreover, the relationship between humans and technology—especially in the context of robotics—will evolve alongside the development of wormhole travel. As we create intelligent machines designed to navigate wormhole environments, the interplay between human and robotic capabilities will redefine exploration. Robotics can facilitate safe passage through unknown realms, enhancing human capacity for exploration while simultaneously raising questions about trust, reliance, and the role of technology in shaping human experiences.

The prospects for adventure and exploration stemming from wormhole technology are nothing short of epic. Imagine embarking on a journey through a cosmic gateway, stepping foot onto a new exoplanet, or witnessing a celestial event that remains beyond the reach of contemporary observation. These grand adventures serve to fuel our collective imagination, captivating generations to come and inspiring future discoveries.

In summary, the implications of wormhole travel for humanity present a complex and multidimensional tapestry. The promise of exploration and discovery coalesce with ethical responsibilities, economic potential, and the evolving relationship between humans and technology. As we stand on the precipice of realizing these possibilities, it becomes critical not only to pursue the extraordinary potential of wormholes but also to remain conscientious stewards of the repercussions that accompany such advancements. In doing so, we can ensure that the journey into the vast unknown enriches our understanding of existence while crafting a future that harmonizes curiosity with responsibility.

11.2. Economic Possibilities

The economic possibilities of wormhole technology present an exciting and potentially transformative frontier. As researchers continue to advance the theoretical and practical aspects of wormhole transport, the implications for economies on Earth and possibly beyond are manifold.

Firstly, the notion of instantaneous travel between two points across the universe could revolutionize industries reliant on transportation, trade, and logistics. In the current economy, the movement of goods and services typically incurs a significant time cost and energy expenditure, which becomes exponentially more complex as the distances involved increase—particularly in the context of interplanetary or interstellar commerce. If wormhole technology were to be developed, the conventional logistics frameworks would be disrupted. Businesses could dramatically reduce transportation costs, streamline supply chains, and ensure that goods reach their destinations within moments instead of months or years. The economic ramifications could extend to consumer markets where prices would likely stabilize or decrease due to reduced overhead costs associated with shipping and logistics.

Furthermore, the industry associated with wormhole travel itself could emerge as a major economic sector. Companies may arise specializing in the design, construction, and operation of wormhole systems, necessitating a workforce skilled in the sciences of physics, engineering, and information technology. Imagine establishing wormhole transit stations akin to airports, where both cargo and passengers would traverse the universe. The construction and maintenance of such infrastructure require substantial investment, presenting opportunities for job creation and economic growth, similar to the rise of the aviation sector in the 20th century.

Additionally, the potential for utilizing wormhole travel in resource extraction becomes an intriguing prospect. If wormholes allow access to distant celestial bodies rich in minerals or resources, interstellar mining operations could significantly reshape how humanity acquires essential materials. This prospect extends not just to elements such as gold, rare earth metals, or water, but also to the possibility of harvesting energy from cosmic phenomena, such as solar flares or tidal forces, efficiently transported through wormholes. In turn, this could lead to a more sustainable approach to resource management on Earth.

The tourism sector may also stand to benefit significantly from wormhole technology. The allure of traveling to distant worlds, viewing breathtaking cosmic phenomena, or participating in scientific expeditions could redefine travel as we know it. Space tourism, currently a nascent industry, could reach new heights, enticing individuals to embark on journeys previously thought to be the realm of science fiction. This burgeoning market could fuel not just economic growth but also public interest in science and technology, inspiring new generations to pursue careers in related fields.

However, with any significant technological advancement come ethical considerations and potential risks. The access to wormhole technology could become a focal point of economic disparity if not handled with careful regulation and foresight. Issues surrounding ownership, accessibility, and governance must be addressed to ensure that this transformative technology benefits society broadly rather than becoming another tool for exploitation.

In conclusion, the economic possibilities of wormhole technology extend far beyond mere theorization. Should it become a reality, the ramifications could be profound, reshaping industries, opening up new markets, and altering humanity's relationship with space and resources. As we gaze forward into a future informed by the wonders of theoretical physics, the exciting potential of wormholes beckons not only exploration but also careful consideration of the pathways we choose to traverse. The implications for human progress, if navigated wisely, could lead to a flourishing economy driven by the quest for discovery and adventure in the cosmos.

11.3. Potential for Scientific Discovery

Wormholes represent a profound intersection of science and speculative thought, opening doors to potential scientific discoveries that stretch our imagination while challenging our understanding of the universe. The concept of using wormholes as conduits for travel has far-reaching implications, not only for how we perceive distances in space but also for the very nature of time, reality, and existence itself. As researchers delve deeper into the theoretical underpinnings of these cosmic structures, the potential for transformative discoveries becomes increasingly tantalizing.

At the forefront of wormhole research lies the possibility of advancing our understanding of fundamental physics. The theoretical exploration of wormholes invites rigorous examination of both general relativity and quantum mechanics, compelling scientists to confront anomalies that could reveal deeper truths about the nature of space-time. As theories evolve, they challenge existing paradigms and inspire new models that could reshape our understanding of gravity, light, and the relationships that govern them. These potential breakthroughs may pave the way for theoretical landscapes previously thought unattainable, encouraging the scientific community to push the boundaries of inquiry further than ever before.

The quest for understanding wormholes could also enhance our search for exotic matter—hypothetical substances essential for stabilizing traversable wormholes. Discovering or creating forms of exotic matter would have profound implications, not just for wormhole travel but for other areas in physics, including the quest for dark energy and the unification of gravity with quantum mechanics. Each step taken in this direction propels the scientific dialogue into new territories, urging researchers to collaborate across disciplines to unlock the ensuing mysteries.

Beyond theoretical investigations, the practical applications of wormhole technology may lead to revolutionary breakthroughs in multiple fields. The possibility of wormhole travel invigorates discussions surrounding human exploration beyond the confines of our solar system, allowing scientists to access previously unreachable planets or moons. These expeditions may result in significant discoveries surrounding extraterrestrial life, atmospheric conditions, and planetary geology. The accumulated knowledge gained could reshape our understanding of biology, chemistry, and the evolutionary processes that may have given rise to life in diverse environments.

Moreover, the use of wormholes could lead to advancements in fields such as quantum communication and information theory. If wormholes can facilitate instantaneous travel or the exchange of information across vast distances, it would not only revolutionize communication technology but would also generate a deeper comprehension of the underlying principles governing the transfer of information in the universe. Understanding how signals could traverse wormholes may reveal new dimensions of quantum entanglement and challenge established notions regarding the limits of communication.

As wormhole research continues, the exploration of these cosmic phenomena stirs curiosity and imagination across various cultural landscapes. The themes woven through science fiction literature and film encapsulate humanity's ethos of exploration and inquiry. The desire to traverse the cosmos embodies an age-old quest for understanding that has propelled societies forward—fuelling scientific revolutions, technological advancements, and philosophical inquiries that define our collective narrative.

In sum, the potential for scientific discovery through the study of wormholes is vast and multifaceted. As researchers engage with the complexities of these enigmatic structures, the dialogue they cultivate enriches our understanding of the universe while pushing the boundaries of what is conceivable. The landscape of discovery opens up new avenues of exploration, accommodating dreams and aspirations that challenge the essence of our existence. The journey toward unraveling the mysteries of wormholes invites us all—scientists, dreamers, and explorers—to transcend the limitations of our current comprehension, turning the headlines of theoretical physics into the foundational texts of future realities.

11.4. Humans, Robots, and Wormholes

Human beings have long been captivated by the concept of transcending the limitations of our physical existence—whether through the realms of science fiction or the frontier of theoretical physics. The exploration of wormholes serves as a focal point for this quest, inviting inquiry into the interplay between human ingenuity, robotics, and the profound mysteries of the universe. As we navigate potential pathways through wormholes, it becomes increasingly clear that the convergence of humans and robots will be crucial in shaping the future of exploration and adventure amidst the cosmos.

Envision traversing a wormhole, stepping into a structure that connects disparate points in spacetime. Such a journey holds the promise of unraveling the mysteries of the universe, allowing us to observe celestial phenomena, engage with extraterrestrial life, or uncover the very secrets of existence itself. However, the practicalities of such explorations demand far more than mere human courage; they necessitate innovative technological solutions that robotics can provide.

Robots would play a foundational role in preparing humanity for the reality of wormhole travel. Before any human ventures through the cosmic gateways, robotic probes could be deployed to investigate the environment and the conditions within the wormhole itself. These intelligent machines would gather crucial data about the variables affecting stability, safety, and the potential consequences of traversing wormholes, enabling scientists to devise strategies that prioritize the safety of human explorers. Collecting real-time data about gravitational fluctuations, radiation levels, and even the impact of exotic matter would establish a more robust understanding of the complexities tied to these cosmic structures.

Moreover, robotics can facilitate exploratory missions deeply rooted in the unknown. Equipped with advanced sensors and autonomous navigation systems, robotic explorers would survey unfamiliar environments on the other side of wormholes—be they distant planets, resource-rich asteroids, or enigmatic celestial bodies. Here, the synergy between humans and robots becomes evident. While robots traverse the terrain and gather data, humans would harness that information to formulate conclusions about the conditions encountered, informing subsequent missions and decisions. Although the dream of interstellar exploration may seem daunting, collaborative missions between humans and robots would pave the path toward turning cosmic ambition into reality.

The integration of robotics into the fabric of wormhole exploration also emphasizes the need for effective communication and interaction between human crewmembers and their robotic counterparts. The design of user interfaces that allow for seamless communication in high-stress, dynamic wormhole navigational scenarios will become pivotal. Advanced AI systems empowered by machine learning would ensure that robots adapt to the environments and conditions encountered, optimizing their exploratory capabilities and further enhancing human understanding during the journey. This adaptability would allow human operators to engage with their robotic partners in meaningful ways, fostering collaboration that mirrors the dynamics of research teams on Earth.

As the journey progresses, the implications of such collaborative adventures ripple across the cultural and ethical landscapes. The drive to explore wormholes transcends scientific inquiry and delves into our collective identity as explorers. The successful navigation of these cosmic phenomena could redefine not only our capabilities in space but also our perceptions of existence and interconnectedness. This exploration poses philosophical questions regarding the nature of adventure, the pursuit of knowledge, and the relationship between humanity and technology.

The prospect of revisiting ancient celestial events or engaging with potential extraterrestrial civilizations introduces an ethical discourse surrounding exploration. The role of robots as the first responders to new environments allows humanity to approach exploration more responsibly, minimizing risks to both humans and potential ecosystems encountered. As we look toward the stars and consider traversable wormholes, the blend of ingenuity and ethical responsibility becomes essential in guiding decisions that shape our future.

In conclusion, as humanity forges ahead into the cosmos with the potential for wormhole exploration, the collaboration with robotics becomes integral to our journey. By marrying advanced technologies with human curiosity and daring, we open expansive pathways into the unknown while developing deeper understandings of our place in the universe. The prospect of adventure and exploration intertwined with the capabilities of robots embodies the spirit of discovery, reminiscent of humanity's enduring aspiration to reach beyond the stars. Through this convergence of human and robotic efforts, we inch closer to unveiling the secrets of the cosmos and fulfilling our aspirations for exploration amidst the expansive tapestry of existence. As we navigate the intricacies of wormhole travel, we stand at the threshold of exhilarating possibilities, poised to take steps toward unlocking the mysteries that lie just beyond our current understanding.

11.5. Adventure and Exploration Prospects

Adventure and Exploration Prospects

The allure of adventure and exploration through the lens of wormhole travel opens up a realm of possibilities that has captivated scientists, writers, and dreamers alike. Imagining the ability to traverse vast distances of the cosmos in an instant inspires visions of humanity stepping boldly into the unknown, confronting the mysteries of existence with courage and curiosity. The prospects associated with such exploration are as boundless as the universe itself, revealing not only the potential for groundbreaking scientific discovery but also the deeper, intrinsic motivations that propel us forward as a species.

Envision standing on the cusp of a wormhole, a cosmic doorway shimmering with the energies of spacetime, pulsating with the promise of new worlds and experiences. This is not merely a theoretical construct drawn from the equations of physics; it represents a tangible gateway to exploration on an unprecedented scale. The very nature of wormholes challenges our understanding of time, distance, and what it means to be human in an expansive universe teeming with possibilities. If we could harness the potential of traversable wormholes, we would not only redefine our approach to interstellar travel but also expand our understanding of life beyond Earth.

Past and present appear to blend within the unique environment of a wormhole, creating opportunities where explorers might witness celestial events as they occur, study planets in their youth, or perhaps even exchange ideas and knowledge with other civilizations. The mere thought of such encounters fuels the adventurer's spirit, igniting a desire to journey through the cosmos. The potential for discovering new forms of life, astonishing alien landscapes, and the untold stories of diverse worlds invites endless exploration, promising to reshape our perspectives on existence itself.

Moreover, the very act of venturing into the unknown carries profound significance. Each journey through a wormhole would reflect humanity's quest for knowledge and understanding—a hallmark of our species. Just as the early explorers set sail toward uncharted territories, so too would modern adventurers harness the power of wormholes to chart the paths of the cosmos. Within this context, the exploration of wormholes serves as a reminder of the importance of curiosity, the drive to seek out knowledge, and the intrinsic human desire to connect with the universe on a fundamental level.

Educational and scientific implications undulate through the fabric of wormhole exploration as well. The pursuit of understanding wormholes would inspire not just astrophysicists but also a diverse array of disciplines—including environmental science, engineering, and even philosophy. Imagining the construction of wormholes necessitates a multidisciplinary approach to problem-solving, encouraging collaboration and fostering new innovations that could enrich technological advancements in various fields. Just as the space race ignited waves of progress across scientific disciplines, so could the dream of wormhole travel catalyze a renaissance of discovery and exploration.

With these exciting prospects come significant responsibilities. Engaging meaningfully with new worlds or cultures requires careful ethical considerations to guide our actions as we explore the universe. The approach to interstellar exploration must be steeped in respect for any ecosystems or civilizations we may encounter. It is not simply about the thrill of discovery, but also about recognizing the impact our presence may have on others within the cosmic tapestry. Striking a balance between scientific ambition and moral responsibility beckons us to tread thoughtfully and reverently as we venture into unexplored realms.

As we build upon the foundation laid by theoretical physics, the potential for adventure and exploration through wormhole travel invites us to reflect on what lies ahead. Each revelation, every theory, and each piece of collaboration strengthens our resolve to continue probing the unknown, driven by the innate curiosity that shapes both our identities and our aspirations. The horizon beckons, flaring with cosmic mysteries waiting to be uncovered, igniting within us the adventurer's spirit that transcends generations. Ultimately, the possibility of traveling through wormholes symbolizes the essence of exploration—a journey not just through space but also through the depths of knowledge, identity, and the enduring quest to comprehend our place in the grand design of the universe. As we stand ready to embark, the call of the unknown resonates through our very essence, urging us to take our first steps into the unfathomable depths that lie ahead.

12. The Philosophical and Existential Questions

12.1. Time and Reality

Time and reality are intertwined concepts that form the foundation of our understanding of the universe. Philosophically, the nature of time—its flow, structure, and perception—invites profound inquiry, particularly within the context of wormholes and theoretical physics. As we delve into the implications of potential wormhole travel, we encounter questions that challenge conventional discourse about the linear passage of time and the very fabric of reality itself.

At its essence, time has been traditionally viewed as a one-dimensional continuum, flowing from the past through the present and into the future. However, wormholes, as theoretical constructs, invite us to contemplate a more complex relationship with time. If traversable wormholes exist, they could offer pathways to navigate not only vast distances but also temporal dimensions, effectively enabling travelers to step through portals that lead to different points in time. This shifts our understanding of reality from a linear trajectory to a potentially multi-dimensional landscape where moments and eras intersect.

As we grapple with these concepts, the philosophical ramifications of time travel become significant. The prospect of journeying into the past or future raises the question of whether history can be altered. If a time traveler were to intervene in historical events, the implications for causality loom large. What becomes of the fabric of reality if actions taken in the past ripple through to affect the future? This exploration of alternate realities poses a challenge to our understanding of determinism and the idea that the future is fixed. Instead, it introduces a model where reality comprises multiple branches—each influenced by the choices made along the timeline.

This notion of alternate histories fuels engaging debates regarding fate and free will. If time travel allows for alterations of past events, do we retain agency over our actions, or are we merely players in a predetermined narrative? The interplay between free will and the possibility of alternate outcomes complicates our perception of choice, suggesting that each decision could potentially lead to the emergence of divergent realities. What does this mean for our understanding of personal responsibility and accountability if every action spawns alternatives? The philosophical inquiry invites us to reflect deeply on the implications of choice within the context of an expansive and interconnected universe.

Moreover, these discussions prompt serious contemplation regarding the nature of existence itself. If wormholes can serve as bridges between different eras or alternate realities, they challenge us to reconsider our definitions of self and existence. Our identities, often understood within the singularity of our experiences, become multifaceted when considering the existence of parallel lives that may unfold according to different choices or circumstances. This invites a deeper questioning of what it means to live a life if duplicate selves exist with separate narratives that may diverge wildly from one another.

The ethical dimensions of exploring these concepts remain at the forefront of philosophical discourse. If humanity were to develop the means to utilize wormholes for time travel, what responsibilities must accompany such powerful techniques? The ethical dilemmas surrounding potential interactions with the past are profound. Intervening in historical events could lead to unintended consequences that alter not just individual lives but the course of humanity itself. How do we balance scientific curiosity— the desire to explore, to know—with the moral imperatives to safeguard the integrity of history? This balance between exploration and ethical responsibility warrants serious contemplation, as we navigate this uncharted territory.

In conclusion, the exploration of time and reality within the context of wormholes prompts a rich tapestry of philosophical inquiry. As we ponder the implications of potential wormhole travel, we are beckoned to confront complex questions about the nature of time, the structure of reality, the interplay of fate and free will, and the moral considerations surrounding our explorations. The philosophical dimensions of these discussions not only reflect the complexities of human experience but also underscore our enduring quest to understand our place within the vast cosmos. As we continue to seek answers in the realms of theoretical physics and philosophy, we will undoubtedly uncover deeper truths about ourselves, our existence, and the integral patterns that connect us all to the intricacies of time and reality.

12.2. Alternate Histories and Parallel Lives

Alternate histories and parallel lives are fascinating philosophical inquiries that stem from the potential for time travel, particularly as conceptualized through the lens of wormholes. The implications of traversing wormholes to alter the past or experience alternate realities provoke crucial questions about causality, identity, and the very nature of existence itself. As we explore these notions, the interplay between science fiction and scientific inquiry becomes evident, inviting us to ponder the myriad possibilities that arise from our understanding of time, choices, and consequences.

If time travel through wormholes were indeed possible, the implications for our understanding of history would be profound. The ability to revisit moments in time could allow individuals to alter events—big or small—in ways that could significantly reshape the narrative of history. The philosophical ramifications of this thought experiment incite vibrant discussions around the nature of causality. If a time traveler were to intervene in a historical event, would the original timeline still exist? Would altering the past lead to a branching of timelines, resulting in a multitude of parallel histories that coexist, each reflecting a different reality based on different choices made?

This prompts the contemplation of alternate histories as competing narratives, where each choice diverges from a central point in time to weave distinct tapestries of possibility. Each alternate history could potentially shape the course of societal evolution, culture, and technology, leading to a rich dialogue surrounding the ethical implications of such interference. Would humanity possess the moral authority to rewrite the past, or would such interventions invite chaos into the established order? These inquiries echo through literary and cinematic narratives, where characters grapple with the nuances of their decisions within the constructs of time travel.

Parallel lives present another layer of complexity to the discussion. If wormholes allowed for the exploration of alternate universes, one where different choices led to diverging outcomes, the implications for individual identity could be striking. Imagine encountering a version of oneself from a parallel reality who made choices that led to vastly different life circumstances. This journey introduces profound questions about the essence of identity—what it means to be "you" if an alternate self exists with distinct experiences, goals, and outcomes. The existence of multiple iterations of oneself could challenge our beliefs about autonomy and consciousness, forcing us to interrogate the very fabric of personal identity.

Through such philosophical inquiries, the concepts of fate and free will recur as central themes. If multiple parallel realities exist, does free will remain a genuine aspect of human consciousness, or do we merely navigate through predetermined paths that diverge at points of choice? The prospect of choosing between multiple outcomes creates a dynamic interplay between determinism and agency, contributing to rich philosophical dialogues surrounding the bindings of fate. These discussions resonate within both scientific and philosophical realms, inviting scholars to interrogate their assumptions about the role of choice in shaping not just individual lives but the trajectory of humanity itself.

Additionally, the ethics of exploring alternate histories brings forth crucial considerations as humanity stands at the brink of new scientific discoveries. The potential to revisit and alter significant moments in time introduces ethical dilemmas regarding respect for historical integrity. Would it be permissible to alter events that define collective identities? How would history and society adapt to the knowledge that our past can be rewritten? The exploration of these questions highlights the importance of embodying ethical responsibility while venturing into the realms of time travel, advocating for a conscientious approach that balances scientific curiosity with moral considerations.

In summary, the exploration of alternate histories and parallel lives within the context of wormholes invites profound reflections on causality, identity, free will, and ethics. As we dissect the implications of traversable wormholes that may reshape our understanding of time, we confront deep philosophical questions about existence itself. This intersection between theoretical inquiry and philosophical contemplation serves to enrich our understanding of the universe, urging us to navigate the complexities of our decisions while embracing the uncertainty and wonder inherent in the human experience. As the dialogue surrounding these questions continues to unfold, the insights gained become integral to our evolving narrative about exploration, existence, and the timeless quest for knowledge across dimensions.

12.3. Fate and Free Will

Fate and Free Will

The exploration of wormholes, with their promise of traversable pathways through spacetime, not only excites the imagination but also critically interrogates the philosophical underpinnings of fate and free will. The very existence of wormholes as theoretical constructs prompts profound questions regarding our agency within the universe. If these cosmic shortcuts allow for instantaneous travel across vast distances—or potentially even time—what does this mean for our understanding of temporal continuity and the consequences of our actions?

Central to the debate about fate and free will is the concept of determinism, which posits that every event or action, including human decisions, is conditioned by preceding events in accordance with the laws of nature. If wormholes enable time travel and the ability to navigate different points in history, they challenge the deterministic view of the universe. For instance, consider a time traveler who intervenes in a significant historical event. If one can alter the past, the linear sequence of cause and effect, which forms the backbone of deterministic philosophy, is suddenly disrupted, creating alternate realities or timelines. Consequently, this raises the question: If individuals can make choices that change the course of events, does that allowance for choice not affirm human agency and free will?

The nuances of this debate draw attention to the paradoxes that arise from potential time travel through wormholes. The classic grandfather paradox serves as a foothold for grappling with issues related to causality. If a person travels back in time and prevents their grandfather from meeting their grandmother, this could lead to the traveler's non-existence in the present. Should such an action lead to their erasure from the timeline, we are left to ponder whether events in the past are mutable, suggesting a degree of flexibility in the deterministic framework, or whether a temporal buffer exists that enforces certain outcomes to maintain a consistent reality. This dialectic between free agency and the constraints imposed by the timeline entices researchers and philosophers to consider the nature of existence itself.

Moreover, the possibility that wormholes could connect multiple timelines introduces the fascinating concept of parallel universes, where each decision leads to diverging outcomes and alternative realities. The existence of parallel lives circumscribes the debate on fate and free will further, as it prompts inquiries about identity across different timelines. Who am I if there exists another version of myself living an alternate life based on a different set of choices? In what ways do our lives intertwine, and how do we define "self" in a multi-faceted universe?

As such, contemplating the ramifications of wormhole travel demands careful ethical considerations regarding how we engage with the fabric of reality. The ethical implications of altering timelines or interfering with historical events bear significant weight, enjoining us to reflect on our responsibility toward the trajectories of lives that extend beyond our own. The potential to rewrite history navigates the uncharted waters of moral responsibility, compelling us to consider the effects of our interventions on larger narratives of human experience.

Furthermore, the collision of wormhole theory with the commitments to free will and fate compels us to reflect on broader considerations —our relationship with knowledge, power, and the consequences of exploration. The entwinement of technology and ethics urges humanity to tread cautiously, recognizing that the ability to traverse wormholes entails complex ramifications for both individuals and societies.

In summary, the contemplation of wormholes necessitates a rigorous examination of the philosophical questions surrounding fate and free will. The potential for rewriting history and accessing multiple realities challenges conventional frameworks and invites inquiry into the nature of existence, identity, and moral responsibility. By grappling with these critical questions, we not only advance our understanding of the universe but also confront the fundamental essence of what it means to be human, urging us to ponder deeply our choices, their consequences, and ultimately the path we tread through the cosmos. In this journey into the unknown, we embrace the profound mysteries and the exploration of possibilities that lie ahead.

12.4. The Nature of Existence

The concept of existence itself has long been a topic of fascination and debate among philosophers, theologians, and scientists. As humanity reaches into the universe with the advent of technologies like wormhole travel, we must confront the profound implications this has for our understanding of existence. At the core of this exploration lies the intertwining nature of space, time, and human consciousness, all of which elevate the stakes of our inquiries into the cosmos.

The notion of wormholes posits the possibility of shortcuts through spacetime, enabling travelers to journey vast distances in an instant or even traverse the fabric of time itself. This capability raises fundamental questions about the nature of reality. Is time linear, or is it a pliable construct that can be navigated like a river flowing in multiple directions? If we can travel back to the past or forward into the future, how does that redefine our experiences of cause and effect? These inquiries challenge our interpretation of reality and compel us to reconsider the foundational principles that govern existence.

Moreover, exploring the implications of wormhole travel brings forth the idea that existence may extend beyond our immediate perceptions. Theoretical physicists suggest that traversing a wormhole could connect us to parallel universes or alternate realities—each reflective of different outcomes shaped by the myriad decisions we make. If such alternate lives coexist, how do we construct authenticity in our identity when multiple versions of ourselves exist, each living out disparate narratives? This complexity underlines the intricate tapestry of existence that transcends individual experiences, inviting a deeper understanding of humanity's collective essence.

The exploration of wormholes further sparks philosophical reflections on the value of knowledge and the human desire to explore. The quest for understanding is not merely an intellectual exercise; it encompasses the inherent curiosity that defines our species. As we venture into the unknown, we grapple with the significance of our discoveries, integrating them into the larger narrative of our existence. Each exploration feeds into the rich metaphor of humanity's journey, highlighting our relentless pursuit of understanding the cosmos and our place within it.

Ethically, the implications of wormhole travel necessitate a responsible approach to exploration. The balance between our intrinsically human curiosity and the ethical responsibilities we hold to protect the integrity of the universe remains vital. As we contemplate the pathways of exploration, we must wrestle with the consequences of our actions and ponder the effects they may have on both familiar and unfamiliar realities. The moral weight of our decisions in this newfound context challenges us to reflect deeply on what it means to be responsible stewards of existence.

In this ongoing inquiry, our understanding of existence becomes not merely a quest for knowledge but also a call to engage ethically with the cosmos. The journey through wormholes—be it through science fiction narratives, theoretical discussions, or real-world experiments —allows us to speculate on the bounds of our understanding while invoking a sense of responsibility to those lives that may extend beyond our immediate perception.

As we explore the interface between science and philosophy through the lens of wormhole research, we embrace the rich tapestry of existence—a journey that unites humanity's curiosity with the infinite possibilities the universe offers. The contemplation of wormholes challenges us to reconsider the nature of time, existence, and the very essence of life itself, urging us to reflect on the role we play in the grand cosmic narrative.

Ultimately, this exploration of the nature of existence, intertwined with the promise of wormhole travel, invites us to continually seek understanding, push the boundaries of exploration, and remain morally attuned to the implications of our discoveries. As we stand on the precipice of the unknown, our inquiries into the mysteries surrounding our existence propel us forward, charting a destiny intertwined with the very fabric of the cosmos itself.

12.5. The Ethics of Exploring the Unknown

The ethics of exploring the unknown, particularly in relation to concepts such as wormhole travel, raises essential and complex questions about our responsibilities as we deepen our understanding of the universe. By standing on the precipice of such profound capabilities, we confront the dual risks and rewards associated with venturing beyond established boundaries in science and exploration. This reflection on ethics involves not only the discovery of new knowledge but also a critical assessment of the potential consequences that accompany our explorations.

One of the foremost ethical concerns surrounding exploration, especially in the context of wormholes, pertains to the implications of time travel. The potential to revisit and possibly alter historical events presents a moral quandary that must not be taken lightly. Intervening in the past introduces the possibility of unintended consequences that could ripple through time, affecting not only individual lives but also the trajectory of entire societies and cultures. For instance, if one were to prevent a pivotal moment in history, what price would be paid in the context of our current existence? Such ethical considerations urge careful deliberation regarding the extent to which exploration and scientific inquiry ought to be exercised.

Moreover, we must consider the ethical implications of interacting with parallel universes or alternate realities that could arise from wormhole travel. The existence of multiple timelines suggests that each decision could lead to diverging paths, creating numerous alternate lives marked by unique experiences. The ethical questions surrounding the treatment of these alternate selves invoke profound considerations regarding identity, autonomy, and agency. Should we engage with these parallel lives? What moral responsibilities do we bear in acknowledging their existence and choices? Engaging with such questions requires an intricate understanding of ethics as it pertains to selfhood and personhood, reinforcing the idea that our actions in exploration can have wide-reaching implications.

The environmental ethics of exploration also loom large in the debate surrounding wormhole travel. As humanity reaches toward the cosmos, we have an obligation to assess the consequences of our actions on any environments we may encounter. The potential to traverse to new planets and interact with extraterrestrial ecosystems invites profound questions about stewardship. How do we ensure that our explorations do not lead to inadvertent harms to any discovered civilizations or ecosystems? The ethical framework guiding our explorations must prioritize the preservation of these worlds, acknowledging that our presence could have lasting impacts on fragile environments.

Moreover, the relationship between technology and humanity presents additional ethical considerations in the context of wormhole exploration. The potential merging of human capability with artificial intelligence introduces questions of trust, reliance, and accountability. As we construct machines designed to navigate wormhole dynamics, we must engage in ethical discourse around the roles of these technologies in our explorative endeavors. What happens when AI takes on responsibilities in exploration? How can we ensure these technologies uphold our ethical values and remain aligned with humane principles during their operations?

To navigate these ethical quandaries effectively, we must cultivate an interdisciplinary dialogue that harmonizes scientific ambition with ethical prudence. Engaging ethicists, scientists, policymakers, and the public in conversations regarding the implications of wormhole travel can help shape the discourse surrounding our responsibilities to ourselves and the universe at large. As we venture into the unknown, fostering a culture of responsibility, reflection, and foresight becomes paramount—ensuring that the pursuit of knowledge remains grounded in an ethical framework that prioritizes respect for all forms of existence.

In conclusion, the ethics of exploring the unknown within the context of wormhole travel implores us to navigate the complexities of our aspirations carefully. The exhilarating potential of traversing cosmic distances invites moments of self-reflection, urging us to consider the broader implications of our pursuits on history, existence, and our relationship with the cosmos. As we approach the possibilities ahead, we must do so with a keen sense of responsibility, illustrating that our explorative journey encompasses not only advances in knowledge but also a commitment to ethical stewardship as we strive to unravel the mysteries that lie beyond.

This intricate balance between the allure of exploration and ethical considerations encapsulates the spirit of inquiry inherent in the human experience—the enduring quest that propels us forward into the infinite unknowns awaiting our discovery.

13. Conclusion: Reflections on the Journey Toward Possibility

13.1. The Road Travelled

The exploration of wormholes has been a journey marked by wonder, inquiry, and a intertwining of science and imagination that beckons us to consider the vast potentials of the cosmos. As we reflect on this journey, we notice the transformative insights gained, from the foundational theories established by pioneering physicists to the speculative narratives spun by authors and filmmakers. Each step along this path has enriched our understanding of the universe, paving the way for deeper conversations surrounding the very fabric of space and time.

As we ventured through the theoretical frameworks of wormholes, from the elegant equations of general relativity to the intriguing possibilities offered by quantum mechanics, we encountered a tapestry woven with scientific rigor and imaginative speculation. The works of figures like Einstein, Rosen, Kip Thorne, and others provided the bedrock upon which our exploration stands, gifting us insights about the potential existence of traversable wormholes and the complex relationships between mass, energy, and spacetime.

Moreover, the philosophical dimensions surrounding wormholes—particularly related to time, identity, and free will—have provoked fruitful discussions as we sought to comprehend what it means to navigate through alternate histories and realities. The interplay between our choices and their consequences raises profound inquiries about the nature of existence itself, fostering a deeper appreciation for our responsibilities as explorers of the cosmos.

As we journey forward, it is essential to recognize the reflections of our present reality, juxtaposed against the future potential that wormhole exploration holds. While significant challenges remain, such as the pursuit of exotic matter and the practicalities of stabilizing wormholes, the advancements made in theoretical physics and engineering provide hope. Each discovery acts as a stepping stone toward understanding the universe more fully, revealing glimpses of what could be achieved as our capabilities evolve.

The narratives woven through science fiction—stories that envision wormholes as bridges to new worlds, alternate timelines, and incredible adventures—echo the aspirations of our scientific endeavors. They serve as vital inspirations that blur the lines between possibility and imagination, urging us to dream beyond our limitations. The cultural fabric surrounding wormholes not only excites the public imagination but enriches the dialogue regarding scientific pursuits, illustrating how both realms can uplift and accelerate our inquiries into the unknown.

As we turn our sights toward the future, it becomes evident that the advancements we make today will inspire the next generations of scientists, engineers, and explorers. The journeys we embark upon and the discoveries we unveil will serve as powerful catalysts, igniting curiosity and ambition in countless young minds eager to explore the mysteries of the universe. The legacies of inquiry, creativity, and discovery surrounding wormholes offer a compelling narrative about our collective quest for knowledge—a quest that transcends individual ambition and reflects our shared aspirations as inhabitants of the cosmos.

In closing, let us remind ourselves that the journey into the depths of the universe is an ongoing exploration—one requiring courage, wonder, and an unwavering commitment to understand not only the cosmos but also ourselves. As we venture forth, may we embrace the unknown, fueled by the infinite possibilities that lie beyond, for the road ahead is vast and filled with the promise of extraordinary discoveries waiting to be unveiled. Through every inquiry, every experiment, and every tale told, we step closer to realizing the dreams woven into the fabric of our existence—a journey toward the stars and beyond.

13.2. Present Reality versus Future Potential

In the landscape of theoretical physics and cosmology, the dialogue between present reality and future potential concerning wormholes evokes a rich tapestry of inquiry and speculation. As we stand on the cusp of remarkable advancements in our understanding of the universe, the juxtaposition of current scientific achievements with the limitless possibilities that lie ahead becomes increasingly significant.

Presently, our comprehension of wormholes is predominantly theoretical, rooted in the groundbreaking frameworks established through general relativity and quantum mechanics. The intricate equations that describe how mass and energy warp spacetime provide the bedrock for the existence of these fascinating structures. While significant strides have been made, such as Kip Thorne's contributions to the understanding of traversable wormholes and the role of exotic matter, tangible proof of their existence remains elusive. The current state of research emphasizes a foundational challenge: how can we not only prove the existence of wormholes but also develop the technologies needed for potential traversability?

The anticipation for future progress paints a hopeful horizon. As experimental physics converges with advancements in computational modeling, the exploration of wormholes could undergo a transformation. Researchers are continuously pushing the boundaries of theoretical inquiry, using virtual simulations to investigate the conditions under which traversable wormholes could arise. Furthermore, as instruments designed to detect gravitational waves and analyze cosmic particles yield new insights, the hope is that they may reveal evidence consistent with wormhole activity. This interplay between theory and evidence fosters an environment ripe for discovery, where the future of physics may hinge on revelations gleaned from systematic investigation and collaborative research.

Moreover, as we chart the course toward exploring the cosmos, the future potential of wormhole travel expands our conceptual framework of space exploration. Imagine a reality where interstellar travel becomes a matter of moments rather than lifetimes, where humanity engages with distant planets and civilizations, breaking free from the constraints imposed by vast distances. The emergence of wormhole technology could facilitate not just a new mode of transportation but also a fresh phase of cultural discovery and exchange.

As we ponder the duality of present reality and future potential, we recognize the ethical considerations that accompany the exploration of wormholes. Foreseeing the impact of our research compels us to engage in thoughtful discourse about our responsibilities as explorers. The ability to traverse through time and space invites reflections on how we interact with the past, present, and possible futures, shaping the ethical frameworks surrounding our journey through the cosmos.

This interplay between current understandings and the aspirations for future exploration encapsulates the essence of scientific endeavor —a relentless pursuit of knowledge driven by curiosity and wonder. The advancements we make today, however tentative, will resonate into the future, inspiring generations to dream beyond the imaginable and seek the extraordinary in our quest to unravel the universe.

As we look forward, the dialogue surrounding wormholes serves as both a reflection of where we are and a beacon illuminating the path that lies ahead. The anticipation of what could be propels us forward into uncharted territories, where each inquiry into the fabric of spacetime reveals deeper truths about our existence and the mysteries of the cosmos. The balance between present reality and future potential fuels our collective ambition, allowing us to envision a future steeped in adventure, exploration, and transformative discoveries. As we continue the journey, the possibilities remain boundless, inviting us to step boldly into the unknown and seek the wonders that await beyond the horizon.

13.3. Echoes of Science and Fiction

The journey towards comprehending wormholes stands as a remarkable testament to humanity's quest for knowledge and exploration. Each step has been marked by scientific rigor, imaginative speculation, and a drive to push the boundaries of understanding. As we conclude this exploration of wormholes and the broader tapestry of existence they inhabit, it becomes evident that the implications stretch far into not just theoretical realms but also practical and philosophical dimensions that shape our understanding of the universe and our place within it.

From the foundational efforts of pioneers in the field of physics to the groundbreaking advancements in experimental methods and interdisciplinary collaborations, the exploration of wormholes has conjured a landscape ripe with possibilities. The theoretical discussions surrounding their existence prompt reflections on time, causality, identity, and the ethical ramifications of wielding such extraordinary technology. Each inquiry into these cosmic constructs fosters a dialogue that enriches both scientific understanding and philosophical contemplation, revealing the intricacies of our relationship with the cosmos.

As we consider inspirations for future generations, it becomes clear that the journeys taken today will serve as the bedrock for the aspirations of tomorrow's scientists, thinkers, and dreamers. The intersection of science and art, the blending of theoretical inquiry with narrative exploration, fosters a rich environment where curiosity is encouraged, and innovative thinking flourishes. It is imperative that we continue to inspire young minds to dream beyond the conventional, to challenge the limits of current knowledge, and to envision futures steeped in possibility.

Ultimately, the journey of discovery continues, fueled by the curiosity that defines humanity. Standing on the threshold of the unknown, with the tantalizing prospect of traversing the very fabric of space and time before us, we invite each individual to contribute to this narrative of exploration. No matter how far our understanding may extend or how profound our technological advancements might become, the adventure lies in the pursuit. As we gaze into the cosmos and treat the mysteries of existence with reverence and wonder, we recognize that the echoes of science and fiction will shape the stories we tell, the lives we lead, and the paths we take into the infinite expanse that lies ahead.

The journey through wormholes beckons us to step forward, to embrace the unknown, and to collect the experiences and wisdom necessary to navigate these realms. As explorers of the cosmos, let us remain guided by our thirst for knowledge while being mindful of our responsibilities—bridging the gap between the present uncertainties and the future potential of this extraordinary canvas we inhabit. The cosmos awaits, and within it lies a spectrum of horizons waiting to be unveiled—each a testament to our boundless human spirit and the infinite possibilities that lie just beyond what we know.

13.4. Inspirations for the Generations

The notion of wormholes has sparked countless ideas about the future of exploration and has inspired scientists, writers, and dreamers to imagine a world where the vastness of space becomes more navigable. This cosmic curiosity transcends mere fascination; it lays the groundwork for future generations to explore not only the physical universe but also the intricacies of existence and time itself.

As current advancements in theoretical physics and experimental methodologies unfold, they stand poised to foster excitement in the minds of aspiring scientists and explorers. Theoretical explorations surrounding wormhole mechanics provide an intellectually rich environment for future researchers to engage with ideas that challenge established paradigms. By delving into the intricacies of spacetime structure, mass-energy interactions, and the possibility of manipulating the very fabric of the universe, budding scientists can be inspired to innovate and push the boundaries of our understanding.

Furthermore, the diverse ways in which wormholes have proliferated in popular culture, literature, and film serve as fertile ground for imagination. Stories that portray the fantastical possibilities of wormhole travel entertain and engage audiences, instilling a sense of wonder and curiosity that can translate into lifelong passions for science and exploration. As young minds are captivated by the adventures depicted in narratives of cosmic journeys, they may feel compelled to pursue careers in astrophysics, engineering, or science communication. The representation of science in creative works ensures that the legacy of wormhole exploration extends to those who will follow, serving as a profound inspiration for the generations to come.

As engaging as these narratives may be, the responsibility of fostering a culture of inquiry must not be overlooked. It is imperative to encourage ethical considerations in the exploration of the cosmos, reinforcing the need to approach new realms with respect and understanding. By instilling values of stewardship in upcoming generations, we can prepare them to navigate the potential complexities of interstellar travel and the ethical questions surrounding humanity's role as explorers.

The journey into the unknown is not solely a scientific pursuit; it embodies humanity's innate drive to connect with the mysteries of existence. This journey spans disciplines and dialogues, bridging theoretical physics with philosophical inquiry. The complex questions arising from the pursuit of wormhole navigation compel individuals to grapple with the nature of reality, time, and identity itself. By nurturing this spirit of inquiry, we can cultivate a generation of scientists, thinkers, and creatives ready to tackle the challenges that lie ahead and guided by a profound desire to explore.

Ultimately, the exploration of wormholes serves as a profound metaphor for the human experience—it reflects not only our quest for knowledge but also our aspirations to connect with the broader universe. As we contemplate the future of wormhole exploration, we must recognize that the journey is as important as the destination. The process of inquiry, exploration, and discovery embodies our collective spirit, inviting every individual to participate in the ongoing quest to unlock the secrets of the cosmos.

In conclusion, the inspirations derived from wormhole theories are profound and multifaceted. With each advancement, whether theoretical or experimental, we inch closer to expanding humanity's horizon of possibilities. The journey of exploring these cosmic structures remains open and inviting, a testament to the limitless nature of curiosity and the potential to chart a course toward uncharted territories. As we embrace this journey, let's inspire the next generations to reach for the stars, explore the unknown, and create a legacy rooted in exploration, knowledge, and responsibility. The universe awaits—may we continue to seek the wonders that lie beyond, united in the pursuit of discovery that transcends all boundaries.

13.5. The Journey Continues

As we draw closer to the conclusion of our investigation into wormholes, the journey we have undertaken elucidates not only the theoretical intricacies of these cosmic constructs but also the broader implications for humanity's quest to understand and explore the universe. The intersection of science and imagination has guided us through a rich tapestry of inquiry that spans the depths of theoretical physics and touches the horizons of philosophy, ethics, and culture.

From the foundational principles of general relativity to the complexities of quantum mechanics, our examination of wormholes has illuminated how these phenomena challenge our conventional notions of time and space. The implications of potentially traversing a wormhole provoke profound questions about causality, identity, and the very fabric of existence. As we navigate these ideas, we invite the next generation of scholars, scientists, and dreamers to join the discussion—imagine the possibilities and challenge the boundaries of our understanding.

Wormhole exploration spurs an innate human desire to transcend the known, to venture into the unexplored reaches of the cosmos. As technology evolves and our scientific endeavors continue to advance, the dream of leveraging wormhole phenomena may become more tangible. The journey into the realm of wormhole research echoes the cries of explorers from ages past who sought to discover new worlds rich with potential. It is an enduring testament to human curiosity and resilience, traits that have propelled societies forward in the pursuit of knowledge.

In contemplating the future, it is essential to reflect on the ethical responsibilities that accompany the ability to traverse the cosmos. The potential for manipulating spacetime raises questions about our role as explorers and our obligations to protect and respect the environments we encounter. An imbued awareness of ethical considerations must guide our pursuit of knowledge as we imagine and enact explorations that expand our understanding of existence.

The echoes of this journey resonate with both excitement and aspiration, encouraging us to remain engaged in the dialogue surrounding wormholes, exploration, and the echoes of scientific inquiry. The interplay between science and creative storytelling will continue to inspire curiosity and ambition, fostering an environment conducive to bridging imaginative worlds and scientific exploration.

As we close this chapter, let us reaffirm our commitment to the pursuit of knowledge. The journey through the realms of wormhole theory is not bound by linear narratives; it is an ongoing exploration filled with discovery, uncertainty, and promise. The adventure awaits as we stand on the brink of what may yet be possible, grappling with the questions that intrigue our hearts and minds.

In this spirit of exploration, we are called to embrace the journey with open hearts and inquisitive spirits, ever ready to take on the challenges and opportunities that lie ahead. The journey into the cosmos, with all its mysteries, beckons us to continue exploring, questioning, and dreaming—one step through the cosmic doorway at a time. To infinity and beyond, for the odyssey continues, filled with wonders waiting to be unveiled.